Reliving Tagore

Poetry, Prose and Perceptions

Ruma Chakravarti

Vitasta

Let Knowledge Spread

Published by
Renu Kaul Verma
Vitasta Publishing Pvt Ltd
2/15, Ansari Road, Daryaganj
New Delhi - 110 002
info@vitastapublishing.com

ISBN 978-93-82711-94-0

Typeset by Vits Press
Printed by Vikas Computer and Printers

Contents

Acknowledgements *vii*
Publisher's Note *ix*

The Year 1400 1
Rain Falls All Day 4
Our Little River 8
Mother, Remembering You 10
By the Pond's Edge 12
The Brave Boy 14
The Market 17
A Dream City 19
Hide and Seek 21
I Will Not Let You Go 23
Divine Hunger 30
The Parable of the Parrot 37
The Guest 43
Post Master 65
The Girl 74
Flower of the Night 78

The Sleeping One 80
Everlasting Love 84
The Ordinary Woman 86
The Two Birds 92
Shubha 95
The Invitation 104
The Flute 109
The Kiss 113
The Accidental Meeting 138
Green Mangoes 141
The Uninvited 145
The Dowry 153
The Living and the Dead 163
The Skeleton 179
Hungry Stones 189
Ramkanai's Folly 206
The Jewels 213
The Final Night 234
At Night 252
Some Time Away 268
In Sickness 270
The Offering 272
The Handmaiden's Prayer 273
Your Conch Shell 278
Unfortunate Land 281
Africa 283
Why, I ask 286
Gandhari's Supplication 288

This book is for all the teachers I have ever had and especially the ones who encouraged me. Not all of these lessons took place in a classroom and not all of you are aware of how you helped. But thank you still, with gratitude and joy.

Acknowledgements

Art acknowledgement: The British Museum holds this untitled artwork by Rabindranath Tagore, which was done in the late 1920s.

I would like to thank my parents and my family for listening patiently, reading critically and being there with the right words when they were asked.

Publisher's Note

Rabindranath Tagore was born in 1861 and to bring his work to a generation of net-savvy readers a hundred and fiftyfive years later is a daunting task. There does not have to be a reason for a new book from Tagore though, his stories are evergreen, his poetry always as evocative, his plays timeless, his perceptions, as relevant and in context now as they were when he wrote his first poem at twelve.

Our attempt in this book is to make our 21st century readers relive Tagore, get a feel for his life and times, his paintings, his romanticism, his obsession with afterlife, his radical thinking, his gender-sensitivity, his connotations and nuances, his rebellion against classicism in art and language, his diversity of thought and feeling, his simplicity of ideas and complexities of presentation, the stories within stories, his perception of caste, class, community, the inconclusiveness in the endings at times. In this collection we try to bring all of this together in just one book, a book that will give the modern reader a glimpse of the literary span Tagore encompassed, avant-garde. And this is not to forget that he continues to hold the position of Bengal's foremost musician and composer for more than a hundred years, his style, Rabindrasangeet/Robindroshongeet, now a genre. He met Gagan Harkara, through whom he became familiar with Baul Lalon Shah (Lalon Fakir), whose folk songs greatly influenced Tagore. Tagore worked to popularise Lalon's songs. Though he was often accused of being pro-British, Tagore's compositions were chosen by two nations as national anthems: India's *Jana Gana Mana* and Bangladesh's *Amar Shonar Bangla*. Some sources say that Sri Lanka's national anthem was also written by Tagore, or that it was inspired by Tagore's work.

We begin the book with a painting by Tagore. He took up painting and drawing at sixty. In 1930, his paintings were exhibited in Paris and London. He was likely red-green colour blind, resulting in works that exhibited strange colour schemes and off-beat aesthetics. Tagore was influenced by scrimshaw from northern New Ireland, Haida carvings from British Columbia, and woodcuts by Max Pechstein. His artist's eye for handwritings were revealed in the simple artistic and rhythmic leitmotifs embellishing the scribbles, cross-outs, and word layouts of his own manuscripts. Some of Tagore's lyrics corresponded in a synesthetic sense with particular paintings.

Surrounded by several painters, Tagore had always wanted to paint. Writing and music, playwriting and acting came to him naturally and almost without training, as it did to several others in his family, and in even greater measure. But painting eluded him. Yet he tried repeatedly to master the art and there are several references to this in his early letters and reminiscence.

In 1900 for instance, when he was nearing forty and was already a celebrated writer, he wrote to Jagadishchandra Bose, 'You will be surprised to hear that I am sitting with a sketchbook drawing. Needless to say, the pictures are not intended for any salon in Paris, they cause me not the least suspicion that the national gallery of any country will suddenly decide to raise taxes to acquire them. But, just as a mother lavishes most affection on her ugliest son, so I feel secretly drawn to the very skill that comes to me least easily'. He also realised that he was using the eraser more than the pencil, and dissatisfied with the results he finally withdrew, deciding it was not for him to become a painter.

Rabindra Chitravali, edited by noted art historian R Siva Kumar, for the first time makes the paintings of Tagore accessible to art historians and scholars. It also brings together a selection of Rabindranath's own statements and documents relating to the presentation and reception of his paintings during his lifetime.

In this edition, we also bring you three famous reproductions of his portraits.

At sixteen, Tagore released his first substantial poems under the pseudonym *Bhānusiṃha* (Sun Lion), which were seized upon by literary authorities as long-lost classics. By 1877 he graduated to his first short stories and dramas, published under his real name. Tagore modernised Bengali writing by spurning rigid classical forms and resisting linguistic strictures. His novels, stories, songs, dance-dramas, and essays were political and personal. *Gitanjali* (*Song Offerings*), *Gora* (*Fair-Faced*) and *Ghare-Baire* (*The Home and the World*) are his best-known works, 'and his verse, short stories, and novels were acclaimed—or panned—for their lyricism, colloquialism, naturalism, and unnatural contemplation', Wikipedia tells our net-loving generation.

One sees the simplicity of his narrative in one of the very first poems in this collection, *Rain Falls All Day.* How easily he could get in and out of a child's mind in *Our Little River* or *The Brave Boy.* At the same time, he was conversant with the situational pathos and relationships, which he demonstrates superbly in poems like *Divine Hunger* or *I will Not Let You Go.*

The evils of caste and religious persecution did not escape him as we find in the stories *The Uninvited* and *The Handmaiden's Prayer,* nor did the evil of dowry, all practices that exist even today. The need for truth and justice continues as seen in the stories, *Ramkanai's Folly* and *Gandhari's Plea,* a play Tagore had written as early as in 1898.

Filmmaker Anurag Basu, filming Tagore's short stories, has commented on his masterful sketches of the 'female' of the species. His understanding of the life of the girl child, the young woman, the burden of rituals she had to suffer in 20th century Bengal, and his championing of the need for emancipation is unmatched, as depicted in his stories like *The Ordinary Woman.* The burden of guilt is sketched eerily in the story, *At Night.*

In November 1913, Tagore won that year's Nobel Prize in Literature: the Swedish Academy appreciated the idealistic—and for Westerners—accessible nature of a small body of his translated material focussed on the 1912 *Gitanjali: Song Offerings.* He was the first non-European to win the Nobel Prize in Literature. In 1915, the British Crown granted Tagore a knighthood.He renounced the title after the 1919 Jallianwala Bagh massacre.

Tagore despised rote classroom schooling. In *The Parrot's Training,* [*The Parable of the Parrot* in this book] a bird is caged and force-fed textbook pages—to death. Tagore, visiting Santa Barbara in 1917, conceived a new type of university: he sought to 'make Santiniketan the connecting thread between India and the world [and] a world center for the study of humanity somewhere beyond the limits of nation and geography'. The school, which he named Visva Bharati, had its foundation stone laid on 24 December 1918.

In 1890 Tagore began managing his vast ancestral estates in Shelaidaha (today a region of Bangladesh). As *Zamindar Babu,* Tagore criss-crossed the riverine holdings in command of the

Padma, the luxurious family barge, and many of his plots are situated on boats. Tagore released his *Manasi* poems in 1890 and this is among his best-known work. The period 1891–1895, Tagore's *Sadhana* period, named after one of Tagore's magazines, was his most productive; in these years he wrote more than half the stories of the three-volume, 84-story *Golpo Guchcho*. Its ironic and grave tales examined the voluptuous poverty of an idealised rural Bengal.

Tagore was cosmopolitan. Between 1878 and 1932, Tagore travelled to more than thirty countries. In 1912, he took a sheaf of his translated works to England, where they gained attention from missionary and Gandhi protégé Charles F Andrews, Irish poet William Butler Yeats, Ezra Pound, Robert Bridges, Ernest Rhys, Thomas Sturge Moore and others. Yeats wrote the preface to the English translation of *Gitanjali*; Andrews joined Tagore at Santiniketan. In November 1912 Tagore began touring the United States. From May 1916 until April 1917, he lectured in Japan and the United States. Shortly after returning home the 63-year-old Tagore accepted an invitation from the Peruvian government. He travelled to Mexico. In May 1926 Tagore met Mussolini in Rome. On 14 July 1927 Tagore and two companions began a four-month tour of Southeast Asia. They visited Bali, Java, Kuala Lumpur, Malacca, Penang, Siam and Singapore. The resultant travelogues compose *Jatri* (1929). In early 1930 he left Bengal again for a nearly year-long tour of Europe and the United States. Upon returning to Britain, he lived among missionaries and wrote his Oxford Hibbert Lectures, and spoke at the annual London Quaker meet. He then toured Switzerland and Germany from June to mid-September 1930, then went on to the Soviet Union. In April 1932 Tagore, intrigued by the Persian mystic Hafez, was hosted by Reza Shah Pahlavi. In his other travels, Tagore interacted with Henri Bergson, Albert Einstein, Robert Frost, Thomas Mann, George Bernard Shaw, HG Wells, Romain Rolland and Aga Khan III. Visits to Persia and Iraq (in 1932) and Sri Lanka (in 1933) comprised Tagore's final foreign tours, open sources tell us.

In translation his poetry was viewed as spiritual and mercurial; however, his 'elegant prose and magical poetry' remain largely unknown outside Bengal despite many translations. Tagore introduced new prose and verse forms and the use of colloquial language into Bengali literature, thereby freeing it from traditional models based on classical Sanskrit. His early works translated into English include *Gitanjali* (1912), *The Gardener*, *The Crescent Moon*, *Vocation* (all in 1913) and *Chitra*, a play (in 1914).

Known mostly for his poetry, Tagore wrote novels, essays, short stories, travelogues, dramas and thousands of songs. Of Tagore's prose, his short stories are perhaps most highly regarded; he is indeed credited with originating the Bengali-language version of the genre. His works are frequently noted for their rhythmic, optimistic and lyrical nature. Such stories mostly borrow from deceptively simple subject matter: commoners. Tagore's non-fiction grappled with history, linguistics and spirituality. He wrote autobiographies. His travelogues, essays and lectures were compiled into several volumes, including *Europe Jatrir Patro* (*Letters from Europe*) and *Manusher Dhormo* (*The Religion of Man*). His brief chat with Einstein, 'Note on the Nature of Reality', is included as an appendix to the latter.

On the occasion of Tagore's 150th birthday an anthology (titled *Kalanukromik Rabindra Rachanabali*) of the total body of his works is currently being published in Bengali in chronological order. This includes all versions of each work and fills about eighty volumes. In 2011, Harvard University Press collaborated with Visva Bharati University to publish *The Essential Tagore*, the largest anthology of Tagore's works available in English; it was edited by Fakrul Alam and Radha Chakravarthy and marked the 150th anniversary.

Tagore reshaped Bengali literature and music, as well as Indian art with Contextual Modernism in the late 19th and early 20th centuries. Tagore died in 1941, at eighty. AK Sen, brother of the first chief election commissioner, received dictation from Tagore on 30 July 1941, a day prior to a scheduled operation, which was his last poem: *I'm lost in the middle of my birthday. I want my friends, their touch, with the earth's last love. I will take life's final offering, I will take the human's last blessing. Today my sack is empty. I have given completely whatever I had to give. In return if I receive anything—some love, some forgiveness—then I will take it with me when I step on the boat that crosses to the festival of the wordless end.*

—Renu Kaul Verma, Papri Sri Raman

The Year 1400

A hundred years from this day
Who are you that sits down to read my poem
Filled with curiosity—
A hundred years from this day.

The joy of this newly minted spring morn. Even a trace of that—
One perfumed flower, one joyous bird song
Just one of the colours that helped paint this day
Not one of those can I send to you, wrapped in my love
For you to hold
A hundred years from this day.

Still I would that you sit once, doors opened to the South
By a window

And looking upon the distance, allow imagination to reign free
Think of how once
On a day a hundred years earlier
A hundred feelings came drifting down from the heavens
To touch the soul of the universe—
On a day of Phalgun, without rain
Eager, intoxicated—
On shimmering wings scented with the
pollen of a hundred flowers
That southerly breeze—

Has surprised the old earth, colouring it again
In a youthful blush
A hundred years before you walked this earth.
On that day, his heart restless, enveloped in song,
A poet kept watch—
How he wished that his words unspoken
would burst forth into bloom
With such love
On a day a hundred years earlier.

A hundred years from this day
What new poet will it be that sings for your pleasure?
I send the felicitations of this spring day
For them to enjoy.

Let my spring song ring across the
firmament of your spring
Even if only for a moment

In the pulse of your heart and in the dancing
wings of your bees
In the rustle of leaf song.

A hundred years from this day.

(1400 Shaal, 14th February 1896)

Rain Falls All Day

The day is almost done,
The sun is ready for bed.
All the skies are filled with cloud
Each one seeks the moon so proud.
Cloud piled upon cloud—
Hue painted upon hue,
In the temple the bells ring
Ding, dong, ding.
Rains pour down on the far banks,
The trees grow wet and smudged.
On this side atop the clouds
Burn a hundred jeweled tongues.
The wind and the rain bring to mind
Those songs of a distant past—

'The rains are coming, drip-drip-drip,
The river will soon overflow its lip.'
The sky is filled with clouds playing catch,
There is no end to this game unmatched!
They visit each country across the land,
No one asks them to go away.
In how many strangely flowered forests
Does the rain stop to enjoy the scent?
Each moment brings a new game
Who helps the rain to dream these up?
When I see the clouds at play
So many memories come to mind,
All the times I hid from sight
In the darkened corners of our house.
Then I remember something sweet
A song that I used to sing—
'The rains are coming, drip-drip-drip,
The river will soon overflow its lip.'
I remember the room so bright
My mother's face wreathed in smiles,
I remember the clouds calling out
And the fear that I felt.
On one side of the bed
There sleeps a little child,
He is a regular terror all day long
There is no telling what he may do.
A boisterous child indoors
Running to and fro while,
The clouds rumble outside

And the world stirs in fear.
I remember how Mother used to say
How sweetly she would sing—
'The rains are coming, drip-drip-drip,
The river will soon overflow its lip.'
I remember the stories of a good queen
And the evil witch who was so mean,
I recall the wrongs that the poor
Beautiful Kankavati had to endure.
I remember the darkened room with a little lamp lit low,
On one wall danced eerily
Many a blackened fearsome shadow.
And outside, as always
Splish, splosh, splish—
The naughty boys listen to tales
They are silent as little mice.
With that I remember
A song of another cloudy day—
'The rains are coming, drip-drip-drip,
The river will soon overflow its lip.'
When did it rain,
Where did it flood?
They say Shiva got married,
But how long ago was that?
Did the day dawn dark and gloomy
With a day grey with clouds stormy?
Were there sudden forks of lightning
And thunder to set you trembling?
Those three girls that he married that day

Were they happy at all, who can say?
Who knows by which river bank,
In what unknown land,
A little boy is being put to sleep
As someone sings the song—
'The rain is falling, drip-drip-drip,
The river will soon overflow its lip.'

(Brishti Porey Tapur Tupur – Shishu)

Our Little River

Our little river flows in graceful loops
The summer heat dries her to a gentle flow,
Both cart and cattle travel across with ease
Her banks are high, her depths are shallow.

The sand bed glitters, no trace of mud
The far bank shimmers with Kash flowers white,
Where flocks of mynas chirp busily all day
And jackal calls rise at night.

This bank shelters sleepy hamlets in the shade
Of ranks of ancient mango and palm tree
At bath times, children swim and play
Splashing water at each other in noisy glee.

Each day as their bathing is done
They catch little fish in nets of cloth
Women take home their pots scrubbed clean
Their washing all done, they return to their chores.

When the rains descend, the river swells fast
Rushing waters raise voice in happy uproar,
The muddy torrent spins in eddies and swirls,
Both banks uniting in joyous clamour
Awake, to join in the festival of rain.

(Amader Choto Nodi – Shahaj Path)

Mother, Remembering You

I cannot remember my mother,
Only sometimes as I play
Out of nowhere and without reason
A tune comes across time to tinkle in my ear
And I feel my mother must speak to me
As I sit and play.
I suppose my mother must have sung to me
As she rocked me in my cradle
But when she left on fading footsteps
She left her songs behind.
I cannot remember my mother
Only in the month of Ashwin
When from the shiuli groves at dawn,
The dew laden breeze brings

The scents of the flowers to me,
Why do I suddenly think
Of that loving long lost presence?
She must have once gathered blooms
As offerings in a little basket
That is why the festive season still smells
Like my mother once did.
I cannot remember my mother
But still when I sit alone
In the corner of my room
And I look through the window
At the blue skies far away
It seems I can sense my mother
Looking back at me in one unbroken gaze.
Perhaps once, in that distant past
She used to look at me in her lap
Today that same love surrounds me
As I look at the skies above.

(Mone Pore – Shishu Bholanath, 24th September 1921)

By the Pond's Edge

Mother, there by the edge of the pond
By the fence of stakes and ferny frond
There I will go to seek exile
There is not a soul within a mile.

There under the shade of the pine
I will build a little hut quite divine,
Upon a carpet of fragrant dried leaves
The two of us can stay by ourselves.

There are tigers there and bears too
But none will dare to come near you
As I will be there day and night
Guarding us both with all my might.

The demons will hide in bushes and shrub
Trying to peep at mother and bub
But when they do, I will be there
Carrying a bow with which I will take care.

When you appear with gifts of food in hand
A vision of mercy at the door
Somehow all the deer understand
As they line up to be given more.
Tall antlers branch above their heads,
Stripes marking their hides of gold,
They all bow their heads in gratitude as they draw close,
ever so bold.

They all understand everything I say,
And have no fear of us anyway
I will stroke them each
As they sit happily within my reach.

On every tree in the Phalsa forest
The fruits grow dark like clouds in the west
That is where the peacock comes
To show us how well he can dance.

The quarrelsome mynahs need no cause,
They drown each other out with sudden noise
While squirrels feed happily, tails held high
From handfuls of grain as they draw nigh.

(Oikhane Ma Pukur Parey – Shahaj Path)

The Brave Boy

Just imagine, travelling to the ends of the earth
As Mother and I take an unknown path.
You ride in a palanquin carried by a few,
The doors parted for you to see the view
While I ride upon a little chestnut horse
Its feet tapping a merry beat upon the course.
Dust from its hooves in flight
Red clouds flying into the night.
The evening is here, the sun sets in the west
I think we have reached the plain with two lakes,
There is nothing here as far as the eye can see
Not a soul wanders that forsaken place.
Perhaps that is why you worry,
Thinking to yourself, 'Where on earth is this?'

But I am there to say, 'Do not be afraid,
Look there, I see the bridge over a dry river bed.'
The place is covered in brush with wicked thorns
Through them the path twists and turns
Not a cow or calf do I see anywhere
They must have gone home as evening fell there.
I am not sure where we are going either
I can barely see anything in this weather.
I think I hear you call me from the litter,
'What light twinkles by the edge of that lake?'
Suddenly all hell breaks loose as we hear,
A great roar from a hundred voices very near.
You cower in fright in a corner of your palanquin
Calling out the names of the gods to save us
While the retinue runs away to hide
In thorn bushes far from the road side.
I pause to reassure you, loud and clear,
'I am with you, why should you feel any fear?'
Each of them armed with stout sticks
They had tucked flowers in their curly hair
I warned them, 'Watch out you wretches!'
If you take another step forward—
I promise you a taste of my sword,
With one swipe I will take your heads.'
That seemed to make them even angrier
As they roared out, 'Ha, ha, ha, ha, ha!'
You whispered, 'Be careful little one,'
I answered, 'Just watch and see what I do.'
I goaded my horse into their midst,

Shield and swords rang in loud contest,
If you saw the terrible things that happened,
In fright your skin would grow goose-fleshed.
So many ran away in sheer dread
Heads were lost and many dropped down dead.
You might think your boy was lost to you
After battling so many desperadoes.
But I return, bathed in blood and sweat
I tell you, 'It is all over, no need to wait,'

You come down from the palanquin
A hundred hugs from your arms I glean—
You smile, 'What luck that you were with me!
What a horrific end it could otherwise be!'
So many silly things happen each day,
Why can't we have all stories end this way?
It would just be like a real book then,
Everyone who heard it would sit up and listen,
Big brother would surely have said, 'How could that be,
Is the little one that strong yet?'
The neighbours would all say with pride,
'Thank your stars! The youngest was by your side.'

(Birpurush – Shishu)

The Market

The bullock cart from the potter's guild
With pots and pans it is over filled.
The cartman's name is Banshivadan
The boy with him is his nephew Madan.

The market is held every Friday
In Bakshigunje where the Padma holds sway.

There is a whole range of things
That every villager old or young brings
Bitter gourds, radishes and purple egg plant
Tidy baskets woven of cane most pliant,
Mustard seed, dried peas, fine flour
Warm wrappers to buy in every colour

Utensils to make every kind of food
Cheap umbrellas too from the city are good
Sticky pots oozing with sweet cane sugar
Where buzzing flies in their hundreds gather
Boats piled high with golden hay for fodder
Brought to market by the farmer's daughter.

Blind Kanai sits among all the coming and going
Seeking alms in lieu of the songs he will sing!
While the local children laugh happily and shout
As all day at water's edge they splash about.

(Haat – Shahaj Path)

A Dream City

One night I saw a dream to beat all dreams
Little Binu was calling, 'Look at this, look at that'
What I saw then was a great clashing of beams,
Calcutta was trundling off, from this end to that.
The houses each walked, like rhinos built of brick
Along ran the doors keeping pace with each window
All the roads uncoil, like great pythons thick,
On their backs the trams rise and fall as they try to follow
The shops and markets climb up and down
Roof terraces go bump-bump, getting quite sore headed
Howrah Bridge crawls, an enormous metal scorpion
Harrison Road follows quietly, very happy to be led.
The monument swings like a maddened pachyderm
Its brick trunk held high above in rage.

My school building walks quickly like a
student at end of term
Our books on Math and Grammar fly away,
hopefully every page.
The maps glued to the walls are getting quite impatient,
Like so many birds flapping their wings keen to be gone.
All the bells in the city ring out every tune they ever learnt—
They seem not to know that it is no longer dawn.
Millions of people yell 'Stop, Stop!'
'What do you think you are doing? Are you deaf?'
But the city listens to no one, it wants to go on a walk
All the pillars and all the walls quicken to the beat.
I think to myself there is little to worry about,
Let Calcutta go to Bombay, see if I care.
Let it go to Delhi, Lahore or Agra without a doubt,
I will put on a turban and pointy shoes, what a pair!
Or if it goes to England, far, far away
Everyone would have to dress in suits, hats and coats
Suddenly I wake to the sound of what I cannot say
Calcutta is still just where it was,
by the river with all the boats.

(Ekdin Raatey Ami Swapno Dekhinu – Shahaj Path)

Hide and Seek

If ever a naughty game I wish to play,
I would hide as a flower in the champak tree
Early each morning, dear Mother, I would sway
On the branches, among every young green leaf.
Then you would surely have to yield defeat.
Would you still know me for your own?
You would call, 'Little one, where are you?'
I would sit, smiling, quiet as quiet can be.
As you go about your daily chores,
I would sit watching with eyes open wide.
When you walk under the tree down the path,
I look and see your hair still damp from your bath.
You will go into your little shrine to pray,
The champak flowers fill the air with scent.

You will never know that is how,
Your little one, his love to you has sent.

In the afternoons, with the Mahabharata you sit
Once you have served lunch to everyone
The tree by the window sends shadow imps
To tumble in your lap, and across your back.
I cast the restless little shadow that marks
The pages of the book you wish to read
You would never know dear Mother,
That is only me gazing back at you.

As evening falls and the cows come home
You will be lighting the sacred lamp
As you walk past, I am done with playing
From tree, I suddenly drop down as a flower spent.

Again, I will become your little one
The one who says, 'Tell me a story'.
'Naughty boy, where were you all day?'
I will say, 'Will not tell you, nay, nay, nay!'

(Lukochuri – Shishu)

I Will Not Let You Go

The car waits all ready at the door, at the midday hour
The autumn sun gradually grows stronger.
Dust eddies on the empty village lane
In the afternoon breeze; in the cool shade of the tree
A weary old woman spreads out her robe
Sleeping, as though a sun kissed night had
Fallen all over, silent solitude its companion—
Only within my house there is neither rest nor sleep.
The month has passed–the holiday at an end.
Today I must go back to that place
Where work waits for me. The household rapt
With packing my presence away in bags,
Securing the memories within boxes,
Busy sounds ring out in each room.

The woman, eyes liquid with pain
That she carries like the weight of a stone,
Still she will not make the time to cry
Not for a moment, in the rush of departure
She hurries around, still more could be
Sent with me; I declare, 'What is all this!
Pots, pans, plates, dishes, bottles
Bedding, boxes, a king's ransom
In existential flotsam
What use of these would I have?
A little I might take, most I will leave.'
To those words of mine
No one pays any heed. 'What if
Suddenly the need arises in that far away place
Where will you find these things?
Golden lentils, fine rice, betel nut and leaf,
That pot with the lid holds something sweet.
Some dry coconut, two jars of good mustard oil
Mango, powdered, and pulp dried to last
A litre or two of fresh milk, rich and creamy
These bottles are all medicines you may need.
There are some sweets in this pot,
Please, I entreat you, remember to eat those.'
I knew then, words of reason would be of no use.
The pile grows taller like a mountain peak.
I look at the clock, and then turn to
Look at her, saying softly,
'And now I leave'. Suddenly she turns
Head inclined as the end of her sari hides
The tears that threaten bad luck.

Outside by the door pensive in thought
My daughter aged four. By now
On any other day she would have been bathed
She falls asleep as soon as she is fed.
Today her mother has not given her a thought
She has been my shadow, silent and constant.
She was watching wordless and unblinking
The preparations for departure. Who knows
What she thought as she sat quietly at the door.
When I said, 'Now I go, Little Mother'
She said sad eyed, dully, 'I will not let you go.'
She stayed where she was, seated,
She did not hold my arm, nor bar the door,
She just stated the rights of love and said,
'I will not let you go.' But still that time came
To an end and, still alas
You had to let go.
Oh unknowing child of mine
Who are you? Where from have you
Gathered the power to say such words,
With such spirit
'I will not let you go.' In all the worlds
Who will you hold back with your tiny arms
What pride, as you protest from your seat
By the door, your tired little frame
All your strength in that heart beating with love.
From that pain, with much fear and shame
The stating of a wish is all that one can do
'I do not feel like letting go.' Who can say?
'I will not let you go.' Hearing this from your lips

Proud declaration of love, Life
Draws me away with an amused smile.
You just look on, defeated eyes brimming
Sitting at the door like a picture,
I came away wiping my tears.
As I travel I see on either side
The fields of autumn heavy with grain
Bask in the sun. The distant line of trees
That edge the road, spend all day
Staring at their own shadows. The river
Rushing past swollen with recent rain.
White cloud fragments, like new born
Calves satisfied and sated, lie across the blue sky.
I sigh as I cast my eyes across the vast
Expanse of tired centuries old bare earth
Baking in the blazing sun.
What pain engulfs this sky?
The whole earth? The further I travel
I hear that one heart rending tune
'I will not let you go'. From the ends
Of the earth to the highest heaven
Resonates that eternal unending cry,
'Will not let you go. Will not let you go.'
All say, 'Will not let you go.' Even the
Smallest blade of grass is held close by
Mother earth as she says, 'Will not let you go.'
Like a flame flickering at a dying lamp
As darkness threatens to swallow it,
It 'Will not let go.'

In this vast emptiness, across heaven and earth
Those oldest of words, the most heartfelt of cries
'Will not let you go.' Alas,
Still one has to relinquish, and still people leave.
This has been happening since time began.
In the stormy seas, stirred by currents of creation
Arms held open, eyes aflame in eagerness
'Will not, will not let go' calls resound
As life rushes on filling the air,
The shores of that sea surge with anguished lament.
The waves breaking upon that shore,
Held back by the ones that follow,
'Will not, will not let go'- none pay heed
No one answers the call.
From all around me today
Unrelenting beats upon my ears,
A sad cry wrung from the heart of the world
In my daughter's voice, as unreasoned
As a child, this plea from its lips.
For ages it has lost whatever it found, and still
It holds its fist closed tight, and still
Like a four-year-old child, it declares full of unravaged pride,
'Will not let go.' Sad faced, teary eyed
Pride destroyed as each moment passes,
Yet love refuses to admit defeat.
And still declares in subdued revolt
'Will not let go.' With every defeat
It still declares, 'The one that I love
Can they ever leave me and go?

Is there any need as anxious as mine?
As endless, as overwhelming as mine
Is there anything on earth at all?
Then pride reasserts, 'I will not let you go.'
And watches as the loved one leaves like a puff of dust
Before a breath, eyes filled with tears.
Like a tree uprooted that falls down
Pride hurt, head bowed. And still love speaks,
'Truth will be upheld. I have received a promise signed in faith'
'Eternal rights will be mine'—strengthened with that
The frail body faces all-powerful death,
Saying, 'Death, you do not exist.'—such proud words.
What can Death do but smile? The troubled love that
Envelops this existence, weighing upon saddened eyes
Like a tearful mist, shimmering with anxious apprehension.
Hope, denuded, weary draws a veil of unhappiness
Across the world. Today I seem to see
Her two innocent arms in fruitless grasp
Surround the universe, in pained silence.
On the swift flood of tears, lingers
One unmoving shadow—
From a cloud of congealed pain.
That is why today, I hear
From the hearts of trees a murmur
Of such anguish, as the burning midday air
Plays an idle game of indifference with dry leaves.
The day passes, shadows lengthen at the
Base of the tree. A rustic tune plays
A plaintive echo upon an everlasting flute.

The earth waits with hair undone in mourning
Amidst the unending fields by the river
One golden moment clasped to her breast
Steadily looking into the distance, no words fall from her lips.
Just like that four-year-old daughter of mine
Sitting silent, at the door.

(Jetey Nahi Dibo – written in Jorasanko, 29th October 1892)

Divine Hunger

The word spread from village to village
The old Brahmin was going on a long pilgrimage
To wash away his sins, where the Ganga met the sea.
Companions flooded to his door
Young, old, men, women and more
All bound for two boats moored at the shore.
Mokkhoda who greatly wished for salvation
Came and implored, 'Respected Sir,
Take me with you. A young widow
Her saddened eyes would not be convinced otherwise.
She kept on asking—a supplication hard to ignore—
'Where do you see the space?' the Brahmin said.

'I fall at your feet,'
The widow wept, 'I will find myself a seat

Somewhere at one side'. He was moved to say yes.
Still a small doubt, he remembered then,
'What will happen to your young child?'
The answer came, 'Rakhal? He will happily stay
With his own aunt. After his birth as I lay
Near death with the fever, Annada saved him
Nursing him alongside a child of her own.
He lives because of her—from that day on,
He has been hers more than he is mine.
A mischievous imp, he listens to none
If I raise a hand to him, his aunt is sure to come,
And tearfully into her arms welcome
Him. No need to worry, he will be happier
With the aunt who he loves more than his mother.'

Mokkhoda rushed as soon as the old man agreed.
To fetch her belongings, whatever she would need.
She said farewell to family, friends and to her elders
She paid respects in floods of tears.
Coming to the river bank she saw, upon the boat seated
Rakhal, who having heard of his mother's journey, had decided
To join her. She cried, 'Why are you here? Tell me!'

Rakhal answered easily, 'I will go to the sea.'
'Go to the sea? Come down right now! Frightful child!'
He said it again, looking on steadfast, 'I will go to sea.'
The more she pulled his arm, the faster he held on to the boat.
Finally the old man said with affectionate pity
'Let him be, let him be, let him come with me.'

His mother, angered, cried, 'I should give you up to the hungry sea!'
As soon as the words fell from her lips, as soon as she heard herself speak
Her mother's heart sank in disbelief and pain.
And keened in silent shame. Closing her eyes
She called on her gods hastily to avert her word
Picking up her son, she touched his skin as if to guard.
The old man called her aside and murmured,
'Shame on you, shame, such words should never be uttered.'
It was decided that Rakhal would go with them
Annada hearing that from others came
Saying, 'Dearest, where are you going!'
'I am going to the sea', Rakhal said smiling,
'I will return Aunty.' Almost beside herself with distress
Annada called on the old man, 'I tell you Sir,
Taking such a mischievous child is foolishness!
Who will take charge? From his birth
He and I have never been separated, you see
Where are you taking him? Give him back to me.'
Rakhal said, 'Aunty, I am going to the sea,

I will be back again.' The Brahmin said pleasantly
'As long as I am here dear,
For your Rakhal, you need never fear.
Now it is winter, the rivers flow calmly,
Many are we in number, there is no danger
Of any mishap on the way. In a month or two
I will return your Rakhal to you.'

At the right hour the boats set off amid
prayers for safe passage,
Women tearfully said farewell from the shore
In the early autumn dew
The village by the Churni glistened too.

The travellers are returning now, their prayers are all said.
In the evening near the banks the boats are anchored
In wait for the tide. All curiosity satisfied,
Rakhal's homeward bound heart craved his own bed
And the aunt beloved.
Water, water everywhere,
His heart gave up in despair.
Smooth, dark, cunning, cruel, sleek
Ravening tongues taste the air with snake-like lick,

Deep water filled with deceit, with a million hoods
It surged demanding with eager roar
The children of the earth, with hungry maw.
Dear earth, affectionate and silent
Steady, constant and familiar
You endure all our whims, and give us joyous dwelling
Green and gentle, wherever one is living
You draw them with invisible arms
Always bewitching, with what immense power
To the comfort of your vast heart.
The restless child came back again and again
In eager tones to ask of the old man,
'Sir, when will the tide return?'

Suddenly the sleeping waters are moved by some
emotion unseen
Both banks awaken to the journey about to begin.
The boat turns its prow, with mild protest
The rope grows taut, with a roar to get
Away as the chariots of the sea enter the river
The tide arrives. The boatmen call on their gods
As they let the boats face north bound homeward.
Rakhal comes to the old man and says,
'Can you tell me please, I will be home in how many days?'

No sooner did the sun set, after some miles
The north wind grew strong and angry.
As the boats neared the Rupnarayan river mouth
A shoal of sand narrowed the boat's path
A duel between the tide and the wind
Agitated and uncontrolled. 'Anchor the boats to the shore'
Cried the passengers many a time and more.
Where is the bank? All around waves maddened with rage
Applaud their own destructive image
With a million hands. Cursing the skies
In foam flecked spite. Far away could be seen
On one side a faint line of distant green.

On the other side the greedy, angry, ferocity of water
Raising its ire at the peaceful setting fire
Insolent in revolt. The boat
Does not heed the hand at the tiller
Stumbling along in drunken disorder
Stupidly. In the bitter winds of winter

And numbing fear, the people shiver
Petrified. Some silenced
Some wail aloud, as tearful pleas upward they send.
The old Brahmin closing his eyes prays
As Rakhal cries quietly in mother's embrace.
Then the troubled boatman calls out to the people, 'Who?

Who has cheated the gods of what is their due?
Promised something in offering, that is why
something is amiss
An untimely storm, such waves! Listen well and know this,
You must keep your pledge, do not trifle
With an angry god!' Upon these words, all
Threw their money and possessions overboard
Without care and thought. And still surged
The waters swamping the boat and all in it.
The boatman said again, 'Who takes back the Lord's treasure
This is the time to stop, think of the future.'
Suddenly the Brahmin said out aloud
Pointing at Mokkhoda, 'This is the one
Promising the gods her very own son
She steals him home.' 'Throw him overboard!'
In one voice demand the people
Rendered by fear unfeeling and cruel
The woman cried, 'Dear Sir,
Save me, save me!' as she held fast
Rakhal with both hands to her breast.
Angrily he muttered and fumed, saying,
'I am your saviour! In anger you lost all
Sense and sacrificed your son, do you not recall?

Now, when the time draws close, I must save him?
Give him up! Fulfill your word, for your lies
Must all these people give up their lives?'
Mokkhoda said, 'I am but a foolish woman,
What I said was in anger, my Fate,
Why would that be true? Do you not know
How untrue that was as soon as you heard me Lord?
Did you only heed the words I spoke dear god?
Did you not hear the beat of a mother's heart?'
But in vain did she plead, as boatmen and pilgrims together
With their arms angrily dragged Rakhal forever
From her breast. The old man closed his eyes
Looked away, hands pressed to his ears
Steeling himself, clenching his teeth. Suddenly
A lash of lightning, a scorpion sting.
'Aunt' the boy's cries fell against his ears like
Blades of fire, the final pleas of a helpless soul.
He heard his own cries, 'Stop! Stop! Stay your hands!'
Opening his eyes he saw first the mother senseless at his feet
And his anxious eyes turned to the writhing waters to meet
The sight of Rakhal, one last look at the waters around him
And then, one last cry, 'Aunt' and he was gone.
Two tiny fists remained for a while, seeking respite from the sky
Finding none, finally they disappear in deep despair.
'I will bring you back' the Brahmin cried, and then,
He too leapt into the waters.
To no longer rise. The sun continued on its journey
to the west.

(Debotar Graash – Kahini, written on 28th October 1897)

The Parable of the Parrot

Once there was a bird. It was uneducated. It used to sing, but it had never read the scriptures. It hopped about and it flew but it did not know what good manners were.

The king said, 'This kind of bird is of no use, for it eats the fruits of the forest and this is leading to losses in the markets.'

He ordered the minister, 'Teach the bird a lesson.'

*

The duty of training the bird fell upon the shoulders of the king's nephews.

The learned men sat and discussed at length why the accused creature was versed in the wrong kind of knowledge.

They concluded that the nest the bird built out of ordinary straw was not enough to hold a great deal of knowledge. Thus the first thing needed was the construction of a good cage.

The pundits went home happily with their grants from the king.

*

The goldsmith set about making a golden cage. This was so amazing that people from near and far came to look at it. Some said, 'This is the ultimate in education!' Others said, 'Even if it is not educated, it got a cage out of all this! What luck!'

The fellow got a sack filled with money as payment. He set off for home in high spirits immediately.

The wise man sat down with the bird to teach it. He took a pinch of snuff and said, 'This will never do with a few books.'

The nephew then sent for the writers. They made copies of books and then copies of the copies till there was a mountain of paper. Whoever saw this said, 'Bravo! This is education if nothing else.'

The scribes had to carry their rewards home by bullock cart. They went back quickly too. From that day onwards there was no more need in their homes.

There was no end to the attention the nephews gave the costly golden cage. There were ongoing maintenance costs. It also needed regular dusting and polishing which made everyone agree, 'This is improvement.'

Many people had to be employed and many other people were engaged to keep an eye on the first lot of employees. This army filled their coffers with fistfuls of cash each month.

They and all the cousins they had of every hue were now able to behave like men of means and leisure.

*

There is need of every kind in life, but there is rarely a shortage of critics. They now said, 'The cage is an improvement, but what news of the bird?'

This remark made its way to the king's ears. He called for his nephew and said, 'Royal nephew, what is this I hear?'

The nephew said, 'Oh Great King, if you wish to hear the truth, send for the goldsmith, the learned men and the scribes and call those who repair the cage and summon those who keep an eye on those that repair the cage. The naysayers are the ones who have not made any profit out of this.'

The king understood exactly what was going on and gifted a golden chain to his nephew immediately.

*

The king expressed a wish to see for himself how the wonderful education of the bird was going. One day he arrived at the classroom with all his courtiers.

At that very moment the gates rang out with conch shells, bells, drums of every kind, cymbals, flutes and gongs. The learned men were loudly reciting the lessons, their sacred tufts of hair shaking with the effort. There was a welcoming roar from the masons, the goldsmith, the scribes, the overseers and their supervisors as well the various cousins.

The nephew said, 'King, you see what a great affair this is!'

The king said, 'Astounding! And so noisy too!'

The nephew answered, 'Not just noise, there is much meaning to all of this.'

The king happily crossed the gate and was just about to mount his elephant when a critic hiding in the bushes said to him, 'Great king, but did you see the bird?'

The king, startled though he was, had to admit, 'Alas! That completely slipped my mind. I did not get to see the bird.'

He came back and said to the pundit, 'I should like to see how you teach the bird.'

He went and saw. It pleased him greatly. The pomp surrounding the bird was so great that it was hardly to be seen. And to tell the truth, it did not seem that important that one saw the creature. The king understood that there was no lapse in the arrangements. There was no food in the cage, nor any water; but the pages of a hundred wise tomes were being stuffed into the bird's mouth. It was unable to open its beak even to shriek, let alone sing. It was truly thrilling.

This time while mounting the elephant, the king told his principal ear-boxer to box the ears of the critic very soundly indeed.

*

The bird grew more and more civilised each day as its life drained away. Its guardians understood that the situation was very encouraging. And yet the bird still fluttered its wings most annoyingly each morning as it gazed upon the morning light, thanks to its intemperate nature. It was even observed that on some days it tried to gnaw through the bars of its cage with its puny beak.

The jailer said, 'What insolence!'

The blacksmith was brought to the schoolhouse, complete with his bellows, hammers and furnace. With a tremendous clanging an iron chain was fashioned and the bird's wings were also clipped.

The king's sycophants made glum faces and shook their heads saying, 'In this kingdom the birds are not just ignorant, they have no sense of gratitude either.'

Then the wise men picked up pens in one hand and spears in another and gave a demonstration of real teaching.

The blacksmith made so much money that his wife was able to buy herself gold jewellery and the king rewarded the jailer's vigilance with a title.

*

The bird died. No one had even noticed when this had happened. The good for nothing critic went about saying, 'The bird is dead.'

The king called for his nephew and asked, 'Royal nephew, what is this I hear?'

The nephew said, 'Great king, it has been educated.'

The king asked, 'Does it flap around anymore?'

The nephew answered, 'Dear God, No!'

'Does it fly anymore?'

'No.'

'Does it burst into song anymore?'

'No.'

'Does it shriek when not fed?'

'No.'

The king commanded, 'Bring the bird to me once, I so wish to see it.'

The bird came. The jailer came with it, as did the guards and the mounted policemen. The king poked the bird; it did not utter a single sound in agreement or in protest. There was just a rustling from the dry paper that filled its body.

Outside the palace, the southerly winds of spring sighed among the new buds and drove the skies above the flowering forests quite mad.

(Totakahini – Lipika)

The Guest

The landowner of Kanthaliya, Zamindar Motilalbabu and his family were returning to his village home by boat. On the way they had moored near a large market town and were making preparations for lunch when a young Brahmin boy came to him and asked, 'Sir, where are you going?'

The boy could not have been more than fifteen or sixteen years old.

Motibabu answered, using the common name for the place, 'Kanthaley.'

The boy said, 'Could you take me as far as Nandigaon?'

The landowner agreed and asked the boy, 'What is your name?'

The boy answered, 'My name is Tarapada.'

The fair-skinned boy was very pleasing to look at. His large eyes and smiling mouth had a delicate gentleness about them.

The dhoti he was wearing was not very clean. His bare upper body was lean and well formed, as though made with great care by some artist who had taken pains to ensure perfection. He looked as if he had been an ascetic in a previous life and his penances had whittled away all excess from his body, taking it to this perfection.

Motilalbabu said to him affectionately, 'Son, go and bathe, for today we eat here.'

Tarapada asked him to wait and joined the preparations for lunch without any hesitation. Motilalbabu's servant was a Hindusthani fellow who was rather inept at cutting fish and other jobs and Tarapada quickly took charge, and managed to cook a couple of vegetarian dishes with practiced expertise. After the cooking was done, he bathed in the river, put on a spotless dhoti which he took out of his bundle, combed his long hair back from his forehead and stood where Motilalbabu was on the boat, a clean caste thread hanging across his chest.

Motibabu took him inside the boat where his wife and his nine-year-old daughter were. Motibabu's wife was filled with affection when she saw the handsome youth— she wondered whose child he might be, where he had come from and how much his mother was missing him.

Soon two places were set for Motibabu and the boy. Annapurna saw that he was not a big eater, and felt that he might be feeling shy. She repeatedly asked him to have some more of each of the dishes prepared but he had decided that he had had enough and it was impossible to sway him. It was clear that the boy did everything according to his own wishes but he did this with such an easy manner that it did not seem like obstinacy. His behaviour showed no signs of shyness whatsoever.

After everyone had eaten, Annapurna sat him down and asked him questions to find out more about his past. She did not learn a great deal. The one thing she did find out was that the boy had run away from home at seven or eight years of age, of his own will.

Annapurna asked him, 'Do you not have a mother?'

Tarapada answered, 'I do.'

Annapurna asked, 'Does she not love you?'

Tarapada seemed to think this an unusual question and laughed aloud, saying, 'Why would she not love me?'

Annapurna asked, 'But why then have you left her!'

Tarapada answered, 'She has four other sons and three daughters.'

Annapurna was pained at the boy's answer and said, 'What kind of talk is that! Does one sacrifice one finger because there are five of them?'

Tarapada was young and his story was short but he was completely different from other boys. He was the fourth child in his family and had lost his father while still a child. In spite of the many children, he was deeply loved; his mother, siblings and all his neighbours showered him with affection. Even his teachers had very rarely struck him in anger and on those few occasions his friends and family had felt the pain just as deeply. As such, there was no reason for him to leave home. Even a sickly, neglected child whose misbehaviour is rewarded with bitterness by people around him stays within an environment familiar to him; and yet this much-loved child had run away from home with a travelling troupe of performers, leaving everything behind without a care.

Everyone searched for him and brought him back. His mother wept over him as she hugged him, his siblings cried and his eldest brother, who was his guardian did his duty by gently rebuking him and then rewarding him with many allowances and presents due to intense guilt. The women of the neighbourhood took him home and gave him many treats to make him settle down. But all these failed, as did love at stopping him from feeling a sense of longing for the unencumbered freedom that was there for the taking, in the world outside his village. Whenever he saw a boat moving down the river on its way to some other land, or a wandering mendicant came and rested under the huge peepal tree in the course of his travels or the gypsies came and built their low shelters where they wove baskets, his mind felt unsettled. After he had run away from home three times, his family and the people of the village gave up any hope of his ever remaining in one place.

At first he joined a travelling troupe of actors. When the manager started to love him as his own son and the other members of the group grew close to him and even the households where they stayed, took him to their heart, especially the women, he just disappeared one day without saying a thing to anyone. He was never found again.

Tarapada was as wary of being tied down as a fawn but was as attracted by music as a deer is said to be. The songs of the travelling group had first drawn him out of his home. His veins resonated and his entire body swayed to the tune. When he was a child he would sit in the soirees calmly, with an air of oblivion so much more suited to grownups that older people controlled their laughter with great difficulty. Not just music; he felt a great restlessness when rain fell on the dense foliage of trees, the clouds rumbled and the wind wailed through the forests like a motherless giant child. The call of kites from the faraway skies on summer days, the call of frogs on rainy evenings, the jackal's howl in the dark of night; all this moved him. He soon joined a travelling storyteller's band under the spell of their music. The leader started teaching him the songs and made him memorise the stories, thinking of him and loving him like the very bird of life caged within his ribs. Alas, the bird learned a few of those songs and then early one morning it flew away.

The final group he joined was a band of gymnasts. There were a number of fairs in the region during the summer months. A few bands of actors, story tellers, poets, dancers and a number of shopkeepers wandered from one place to another by boat through rivers. The previous year a little group of gymnasts had joined the pleasures of this travelling fair. Tarapada had started by selling *paan* or betel leaf refreshments to people. Later on, his natural curiosity led him to join the group, attracted by the astonishing physical agility of the boys. He had learned to play the flute very well by practicing it on his own—thus his only job during his time there was to play Lucknavi tunes on it while the show was on.

This was the group he had lately fled from. He had heard that the landowner in Nandigram was starting an amateur theatre group—he had been preparing to go to Nandigram with his little bundle of belongings when he met Motibabu.

Even though Tarapada had spent time with many groups, this had not changed his natural inclination for imagination. His soul was completely untouched and free. He had heard as well as seen much that was unlovely, but these had never affected his mind in the slightest. This youth noticed nothing. Like all other ties he had shrugged off, the necessary routine of existence too had left his mind unfettered, allowing him to swim above the murky waters of daily life like a snowy white swan. That is why a clear unlaboured freshness radiated from this runaway child's face, which had made the worldly Motilalbabu invite him to join them without any questions or doubts.

The boat set off when everyone had eaten. Annapurna asked the youth about his home and his family with great affection; Tarapada gave very brief answers to these and finally escaped outside. The river was brimming with seasonal rain and seemed to be teasing Mother Nature with its exuberant high spirits. In the clear unclouded sunshine, the half submerged tall grass plumes at the river's edge, the lush dense sugarcane fields above them, and further behind these, the blue tree line smudging the faraway horizon... all seemed to have woken to the touch of a golden wand. The earth had now decided to unveil its freshly woken beauty before the enchanted gaze of the silent blue sky and everything seemed alive, shimmering with life, kissed by sunlight, newly made, plentiful.

Tarapada went and sat in the shade of the mast. As the boat moved, lowlying green fields, flooded plantings of jute, the waves of dark emerald Aman rice, the narrow paths leading to the villages from the river banks and the villages shaded by the dense forest of trees passed before his eyes. This water, this land, the sky, the activity, liveliness and sounds all around, the undulating landscape and the vast uncaring panorama of the eternal unblinking wordless universe— these were the real friends the boy had; and yet they did not try to hold him down even once with loving arms. He watched with an ever-inquisitive untiring interest as calves ran spiritedly about the bank, with their tails raised high, a horse tethered by its front legs hobbled around grazing, kingfishers swooped suddenly from the fishermen's stakes to dive into the water noisily and catch fish, children splashed around, women laughed and talked loudly as they bathed in chest-deep water and washed their clothes, fishmongers bought fish from the fishermen— nothing seemed to satisfy his need to see more and more. Tarapada gradually started talking to the boatmen. Occasionally, he would help them to row by picking up the punt pole and pushing the boat along; when they needed a smoke he was there to take over—he even moved the sails when they needed to be shifted.

Annapurna asked him before twilight, 'what do you eat at night?'

Tarapada said, 'whatever I get, I do not get to eat every night.'

Annapurna was slightly hurt by the handsome youth's ambivalence about accepting hospitality. She greatly wished to satisfy this homeless wanderer with food and care. But she was unable to find out what would make him happy. She summoned her servants and made a fuss over getting milk and sweets from the village. Tarapada ate well but drank no milk. Motibabu, who was normally reticent by nature, also requested him to have some milk; he answered simply, 'I do not like it.'

A couple more days passed on the river. Tarapada did his share of cooking, shopping for food and even navigating the boat with willingness and speed. Whenever a sight presented itself, he cast his curious eyes on it; whenever there was a job to be done; he was keen to do it. His eyes, hands and mind were constantly on the move and this made him like the scenery around them, ever serene, unhurried, and yet always drawn to action. Every human has a unique position; but Tarapada was a joyous wave dancing upon the eternal waves of the blue, tied neither to the future nor the past, seemingly his one task was to move forward.

He had learned many amusing skills through his contact with many different groups. Untouched as he was by worries, he remembered everything he experienced with astonishing clarity. The tales of the village storytellers, the religious songs called *keertans*, the dialogues of plays—he knew all these by heart. Motilalbabu was reading the Ramayan to his wife and daughter as was his longtime habit in the evenings. Just as he started reading the part about the sons of Ram, Lav and Kush, Tarapada was unable to contain his enthusiasm and came down from the roof of the boat saying, 'Put your book down. I will sing the songs of Lav and Kush, listen to me.'

He then started his song. His clear voice sang sweetly of the rich alliterations of Dashu Ray's songs in perfect harmony and without pause. The boatmen and others came and stood there as an incredible fountain of melody, happiness and compassion flowed across that riverbank in the twilight hour and the two shores stopped all activity to curiously listen, while the passengers of the boats that passed them grew anxious for the few moments as they were able to hear his voice; when it was over, they all seemed to sigh sadly that it had ended so soon.

Moist-eyed, Annapurna wanted to seat him upon her lap, embrace him and breathe in the perfume of his hair. Motilalbabu kept thinking that if he could only keep this youth close the absence of a son would be forgotten. The only one with jealousy and hatred in her hearts was the little girl, Charushashi.

Charushashi was the only child of her parents, the only heiress to all their affection. There was no end to her whims and demands. She had independent opinions on what she ate, how she dressed and how her hair would be done, but these were liable to change at any time. On the days that they had an invitation to attend, her mother would be afraid that she would demand something impossible regarding how she wanted to dress. If ever her hair was not done to her liking, she would undo it and be dissatisfied with everything done to the hair, before finally resorting to floods of tears. Everything about her was like this. At other times when happy, she would be amenable to everything. She would hug and kiss her mother and laugh and talk to her with an excess of love. This little girl was a difficult riddle.

This girl started to hate Tarapada intensely in her mind with all the passion of her uncontrollable heart. She also made life unbearable for her parents in every way. She pushed her plate away in tears while eating, claiming the food was not tasty enough and she hit her maid in addition to complaining about everything without reason. The more Tarapada's talents amused her and the others, the angrier she became. She was reluctant to admit that Tarapada had any good qualities at all and yet when she received proof of them she became even more dissatisfied. The day that Tarapada sang about Lav and Kush, the sons of Ram, Annapurna thought, 'Music soothes the beast of the forest, surely today my daughter will be happy,' and asked her what she thought. Charu answered by shaking her head violently, as if to say she had not liked any of it and was unlikely to ever like it.

Seeing that Charu felt jealous, her mother stopped showing Tarapada any affection in front of her. When she would have an early dinner and go to sleep in the evenings, Annapurna would come and sit near the door of the cabin while Motibabu and Tarapada sat outside and the boy would sing at her request. As his song rang out in the vast darkness around them, the sleeping village would be silenced in awe and Annapurna's gentle heart would fill with a feeling of love and beauty. Suddenly Charu would come there with quick footsteps and angrily say, 'Mother, you are all making such a noise, I am unable to sleep.' She found it quite intolerable that her parents had sent her off to bed by herself and were enjoying Tarapada's singing. Tarapada himself used to greatly enjoy the natural sharpness of this bright-eyed girl. He tried to make friends with her by telling her stories, singing to her, playing the flute for her but to no avail. Only when Tarapada took a dip in the river at noon, his fair skinned beautifully shaped body moving easily through the water like a young water god, did she feel greatly curious. She would wait for the event and even though she did not let anyone know about this interest, she would practice her knitting with a great pretence of concentration while contemptuously looking his way every now and again.

The boat left Nandigram behind but Tarapada did not seem to mind. The large boat moved at a very slow speed, sometimes with the sails unfurled, sometimes with the men rowing down many rivers and their tributaries. The days of its passengers too passed in peace with the beauty of nature and her variety surrounding them like a gentle conversation. No one was in any kind of a hurry and much of time was spent each noon over bathing and meals. As soon as evening fell, they would anchor the boat near a large village, next to the forests on the shore where fireflies glittered and the cicadas sang.

After ten days had passed like this, the boat finally reached Kanthaliya. Palanquins and horses had been sent to receive the landowner and his guards made the raucous crows of the village even noisier by firing off blanks in celebration of his arrival.

While all this was happening, Tarapada had quickly left the boat and had taken a walk around the village. Within a couple of hours he had made friends with the whole village, calling some his brothers, others his uncle, and finding a plethora of sisters and aunts in the female population. This boy could make friends with such amazing ease and speed only because he had no real ties with any one. Within a few days he had won every heart in the village.

The reason he could win people over so easily was that he mixed with them on their own terms. He was not bound by any beliefs but had a natural and easy inclination to take part in any situation he came upon. With children, he was a child but separate and better than them, with elders he was not quite a child, yet he was never precocious in any way, with the cowherds he was one of them, but apart in being a Brahmin. He helped everyone in every task with a sense of familiarity, both with them and the job. If he was in the sweet shop and the sweetmaker asked him to wait for a while, he would pick up a sal leaf and start fanning the flies off the sweet sandesh. If they had asked him to help in making sweets, he knew something of that too, and also a little of how the potter's wheel worked.

He made the whole village his own, except for one jealous village girl. The more she prayed for him to be sent away on a faraway exile, the longer he seemed to be spending in the village.

But Charushashi soon proved that even as children it is very hard to understand the mystery that is a woman.

The Brahmin cook's daughter Shonamoni had been widowed at the age of five. She was Charu's age and therefore her friend. When Charu returned to the village, she was ill and had been unable to meet Charu. When she was well again and came to see Charu, the two friends nearly had a disagreement for hardly any reason at all.

Charu had started to tell a story with a great deal of embellishment. She had thought that she would astonish her friend with an account of how they had found the newly-acquired treasure named Tarapada. But when she heard that not only was he not unknown to Shonamoni, he also called her mother aunt and Shonamoni called him her elder brother—when she heard that not only had he entertained mother and daughter by playing tunes from the *keertan*s on his flute but had also made a flute just like his own for Shonamoni and had on many occasions picked flowers from the thorniest branches and fruits from the tallest trees for her—Charu felt as though someone had pierced her heart with a hot spike. Charu had thought Tarapada was only theirs, to be hidden away and divulged sparingly to ordinary human beings but never allowed to become familiar, so that people would be amazed at his qualities and thank Charu and her family. Why had this amazingly rare creature become so close to Shonamoni? She thought that if they had not brought him with them with such care or looked after him so well, it would have been impossible for Shonamoni and her mother to have seen him. Elder brother indeed! Her skin crawled and burned in anger.

Who would have known that she wanted to have him to herself, that same Tarapada who she tormented continually, who she intensely disliked?

That same day, she had a terrible quarrel with Shonamoni over another minor issue and they parted ways. She then went to Tarapada's room and found his beloved flute which she then proceeded to break by stamping on it.

While Charu was angrily engaged in this destructive act, Tarapada entered the room. He was amazed to see her enraged appearance and asked, 'Why are you breaking my flute?' Flushed and red-eyed with anger, she answered, 'Because I want to, why else!' and before leaving the room she needlessly kicked the already broken instrument a few times and broke into anguished tears before she left the room. Tarapada picked up the flute and found it was damaged beyond repair.

He could not control his laughter any longer over the sudden disaster that had befallen his old, blameless flute for no real reason. Each day Charu became more of an object of great curiosity for him.

Another object of curiosity for him was the hoard of illustrated English books in Motilalbabu's library. He had seen much of the outside world, but he soon found that he could not enter this world of pictures at all. He tried to compensate much of this with his imagination but this did not satisfy his mind.

Motilalbabu noticed this interest in the picture books and asked him one day, 'Do you want to learn English? That will help you understand the meanings of these pictures.'

Tarapada immediately answered, 'Yes.'

Motibabu was very pleased and employed Ramratanbabu, the headmaster of the local Entrance School, to teach the boy English each evening.

Tarapada started learning English with his natural and acute ability to recall and intent concentration. It was like entering an unknown and inaccessible land and he was no longer in contact with his old life. The local people never saw him anymore and when he rapidly strode the lonely riverbanks just before twilight reciting his lessons, a loyal band of local youths would watch him respectfully from afar with some unhappiness, never daring to disturb him in his studies.

Charu did not get to see him much either these days. In the past, Tarapada used to eat in the inner quarters under Annapurna's loving eye—but since that resulted in delays quite frequently, he had arranged for his meals to be sent to him by talking to Motibabu. Hurt, Annapurna had protested but Motibabu was extremely pleased with the boy's interest in studies and had agreed.

Suddenly Charu declared that she too, 'would learn English.' Her parents dismissed this proposal from their whimsical daughter with affectionate smiles initially but soon the smiles were met by torrents of tears. Eventually the parents weakened out of love and acquiesced. Charu joined Tarapada in his lessons with the tutor.

But studying did not come naturally to this restless girl. She learned nothing herself and disturbed Tarapada in his endeavours. She fell behind, never studied and yet would not agree to come second to him. When Tarapada finished one lesson and started on another ahead of her, she became very angry and even resorted to tears. When he finished one book and bought another, she demanded to be given that book too. Tarapada used to spend his leisure hours in his room studying but this was unbearable to this jealous girl. She would secretly go to his room, pour ink on his exercise books, steal his pens and even tear out the pages he was supposed to study in his texts. Tarapada bore all her tantrums with humour, unless it was unbearable in which case he would hit her. But nothing he did seemed to control her behaviour.

He found out a way to control her quite unexpectedly. One day, while an extremely annoyed Tarapada sat in solemn despair after tearing up his inked exercise book, Charu came to the door and thought she would get a beating. But it did not seem like it as he sat there without saying a word. She walked around the room and indeed came so close to him that he could easily have given her a slap if he had so wished.

He did no such thing however, and remained unsmilingly seated as he had been before. She now had a problem. She had never learned how to ask for forgiveness and yet her young heart was extremely eager to be forgiven by her friend. Eventually she decided to resort to sitting very close to Tarapada and writing in big letters on a piece of the torn book, 'I will never smear ink on your pages again.' Once it was written she tried to draw his attention to it in various ways. Tarapada could no longer keep up any pretence at being serious and laughed out aloud. She then became furious and ashamed and ran from the room. She felt that the only way to relieve her extremely heartfelt outrage would be to make the piece of paper on which she had admitted her own guilt vanish from the world for all time.

In the meantime, Shonamoni had timidly looked in on the studyroom a couple of times and had gone away. She was very close to her friend Charushashi in all matters but where Tarapada was concerned, she regarded Charu with great fear and suspicion. Shonamoni would pick a time when Charu was certain to be in the inner quarters to cautiously come and visit Tarapada; as she stood outside his door, Tarapada would raise his face from his book and ask affectionately, 'How are you Shona? How is my aunt?'

Shonamoni said, 'You have not been to our house for many days, Ma has asked you to go there once. She has not visited you because her back pain has been troubling her.'

Some days Charu would suddenly arrive on the scene. Shonamoni was always startled by this. It seemed as though she had tried to steal something belonging to her friend. Charu would raise her voice to its loudest, roll her eyes fiercely and grind out, 'what is going on here Shona? If you are here to distract him, I will tell my father immediately!'

It was as though she was Tarapada's ancient guardian; her only duty to ensure that he was never distracted from his studies in the slightest. But both she and Tarapada knew why she had come to the study room at this untimely hour. Terrified, Shonamoni would make a hundred false excuses until Charu disgustedly labeled her a liar. She then left ashamed and defeated, her fear adding to the pain in her heart as she went away. Compassionate Tarapada would call her and say, 'Shona, today I will go to your house in the evening.' Charu would hiss like a snake, saying, 'Of course you will! Don't you have to study? Don't think I cannot tell the teacher about this!'

Tarapada was unmoved by these restrictions and did go to the old cook's house some days after evening had fallen. On the third or fourth such occasion, Charu did not merely issue empty threats but locked Tarapada in his room quietly from the outside. She then padlocked the door with the lock belonging to her mother's spice chest. After leaving him imprisoned for the whole evening, she finally allowed him his freedom at dinner time. Tarapada was angry and attempted to leave instead of eating. She was then overcome by repentance and repeatedly pleaded with him, 'Please, I will never do this again. Please eat, I beg your forgiveness at your feet.' When he still seemed determined to leave, she wept pitiably and Tarapada was finally dissuaded from leaving and decided to have his food.

Charu had made many promises to herself that she would behave well with Tarapada and would never annoy him ever again, but her temper was ruffled whenever Shonamoni and the others were around and she was completely unable to control herself when that happened. Whenever she had a few days of calm good nature, Tarapada would grow apprehensive and prepare for a tremendous outburst. It was impossible to say which direction this attack would come from. After that came a terrible storm of emotions, floods of tears rained down and then serene peace reigned all around.

Two years passed in this fashion. Tarapada had never yielded to anyone for so long. Possibly he had been tied down by his great desire to study; his nature was also undergoing changes along with the changes brought by puberty which made him more inclined to enjoying a settled domestication. It could even be that the constant onslaught of attention from his companion had ensnared him, without anyone noticing this happening.

On the other hand, Charu was already eleven years old. Motibabu had found a number of good matches for his daughter. He put a stop to her going to the outer house and to her English lessons as she was now of marriageable age. Charu created a great uproar over these changes to her daily routine.

'Why are you looking for a boy all over the country? Tarapada is a fine boy. And your daughter is also fond of him,' said Annapurna one day.

Motibabu was amazed. He said, 'How can that even be? We know nothing of his parents. She is my only daughter! I want to give her away to a good family.'

One day members of the zamindar family of Raydanga came to see her. Her parents attempted to dress her up and send her to them. She locked the doors to her bedroom and refused to come out. Motibabu pleaded with her for a long time from outside; eventually even threatening her with consequences but to no avail. In the end, he had to lie to the guests saying his daughter had fallen violently ill and would not be seeing anyone that day. They went away thinking the girl had a physical defect which prevented her from being brought out to face their close scrutiny.

Motibabu started thinking that Tarapada was a good match in all respects; with him as son-in-law there would be no need to send his daughter away to another house. He also thought no matter how much he and his wife ignored her ill-mannered obstinacy, her misbehaviour would seem inexcusable in the eyes of others.

The parents discussed this at length and sent people to Tarapada's village to find out about his family. They brought news of a good family which had lately fallen on hard times. Motibabu then presented his proposal to the boy's mother and brother. They were very happy to hear the news and promptly gave their consent.

Meanwhile in Kanthalia, Motibabu and Annapurna discussed the day and time of the wedding but Motibabu, who was a naturally cautious man, kept it secret from others.

But Charu could not be restrained. She would suddenly descend upon Tarapada's study room like the Maratha horde. She would raise waves in the solitude surrounding his reading with displays ranging from anger, to love or dislike. This had lately started affecting the free-spirited youth yearning for a few moments of exquisite excitement.

The person whose light spirit had always floated along the crests of the waves of time blithely would sometimes become unmindful and find himself tangled in a varied web of daydreams. Some days, he would leave his studies and turn the pages of the picture books in Motibabu's library where his imagination now wove more colourful and vivid images than those he had conjured up before. He could not tease Charu as he had done previously when she had behaved erratically, nor did he feel like hitting her when she was naughty. This change in him—this feeling of being in thrall and being bound—was like a new dream to him.

Motibabu fixed a day in the month of Shravan for the happy event and sent for Tarapada's mother and his brothers but did not let him know of this. He asked his agent in Kolkata to organise the military band to play music at the wedding and sent lists of all the things that would be required.

The sky was overcast with the clouds heralding the start of the new rainy season. The river in the village had nearly dried up, with waterholes here and there filled with muddy water where small boats were moored. The deep ruts of bullock carts that had used the paths marked the dry river bed. And then suddenly, like Parvati returning home to her parents, a fast flowing stream of water arrived out of nowhere, bringing laughter and music to the empty heart of the village—naked children noisily danced around on her banks, jumping again and again into the water, as if to hug her, the women come from their huts to greet their friend again—the dry lifeless village awakened to the touch of a great life force. Boats of many sizes came laden with things from other places near and far and each evening the banks of the market rang to the songs of foreign boatmen. The villages on each bank spent the whole year with their own affairs alone and with the rains the vast outer world came bearing many gifts for the gentle women on chariots of ochre water. For a few days they were exalted by their ties to that world where everything was in motion, alive and awake. Sounds and words from faraway places came and filled the skies of these silent spaces.

This was just before the famous Ratha fair was held by the Nagbabus of Kurulkata. Tarapada went to the moonlit river bank and saw the boats all leaving with the tide, some carrying the Ferris wheel, some the performing troupes, others laden with things to sell. The musical group from Kolkata had started playing some fast rhythm very loudly and the actors were singing their parts to the accompaniment of violins and emphasizing the beat with a loud roar; while the boatmen from the west raised a cacophony of sound with their gongs and cymbals—there was no end to the excitement. As he watched, a great flotilla of clouds moved across the sky from the east, hiding the moon. The east wind blew hard, moving cloud after cloud, the river rose steadily, in joyful splashing—the darkness pooling in the forests on its banks, where frogs croaked and crickets sang loud enough to saw right through the darkness. It was as though the whole world was staging a festival of motion—wheels were turning, flags were flying, the earth trembled, the clouds moved, the wind blew, the river flowed, the boats floated, songs were sung, thunder rumbled in the clouds, the lightning split the sky again and again, and the smell of torrents of rain came to him from somewhere dark and far away. Only the village of Kanthaliya kept on sleeping in silence with their doors barred against all this somewhere on the banks of this same river.

The next day, Tarapada's mother and his brothers arrived in Kanthaliya. The day after that three large boats filled with various things from Kolkata came and moored at the landowner's own jetty. The following day, Shonamoni fearfully went and stood at Tarapada's study room door very early in the morning, with a little preserved mango wrapped in newspaper and some pickles in a leaf twist but he was no longer there on that day. Before affection, love and friendship could swallow him up completely, this boy who had stolen the hearts of the entire village had chosen to leave, and had vanished once again into the wide embrace of mother earth.

(Atithee – Golpo Guchcho)

Post Master

The postmaster's very first posting was at a small village called Ulapur. There was an indigo mill close by and the indigo planter had managed to get the post office established after much effort.

Upon arriving at the remote village, the postmaster who was a Calcutta boy felt very much the same way a fish does when it is brought onto land. His office was in a large dark thatched hut close to a hyacinth infested pond which was surrounded by undergrowth. The staff that worked for the planter had little time for him and was hardly the right sort of company for a decent man.

Being from Calcutta, he was not great at socialising either. When he was among strangers, he was either insolent or ill at ease and this was the reason why he did not have much interaction with the locals. Yet, apart from his attempts to write the occasional poem or two, he did not have much else to occupy himself with. These poems seemed to describe an idyllic existence filled with the day-long rustle of leaves and time spent gazing at the clouds—all pointing at a very happy life, but the Creator knew that if the genie from the Arabian Nights were to come and remove all the trees overnight and replace them with roads and rows of buildings that blocked the clouds from sight, this depressed gentleman would have come back to life.

The post master's salary was very poor. He had to cook his own meals and an orphaned girl from the village came to do the housework in exchange for some food. The girl was called Ratan. She was about twelve or thirteen years old. There was not a lot of hope of her marriage ever taking place.

When the smoke curled up from the cowsheds of the village in the evenings, crickets called in the bushes and the intoxicated 'baul' singers of the far away hamlets sang loudly to the accompaniment of cymbals and drums—when the poet's heart inside the postmaster beat a little faster at the tremble of trees in the darkened courtyard where he sat—he would light a faltering lamp in the corner of his room and call out, 'Ratan.'

Even though she always waited for this call, she never came immediately and would ask, 'What? Babu, why are you calling?'

'What are you doing?' The postman would ask.

'I was going to go to light the cooking fires—'

'Do that later;' he would say, 'bring me some tobacco first.'

So Ratan would soon enter, with her cheeks puffed from her efforts to keep the pipe alight. The postmaster would take it from her hands and ask in an abrupt manner, 'Tell me Ratan, do you remember your mother?' There were many things and while she remembered some of them, others she did not. Her father had loved her more than her mother and she remembered a few things about him. She remembered some of those evenings when he used to come home exhausted—those evenings were as clear as pictures in her mind and as she and the postmaster spoke, she would gradually sink down on the floor at his feet. She recalled the little brother she once had—on a rainy day many years ago they had stood together on the edge of a pond, pretending to catch fish with a rod made from a broken branch—she remembered this far better than many other important things. All this talk meant that occasionally it would get quite late and the postmaster would no longer feel like cooking. There were always some leftovers from the morning and Ratan would quickly light the fire and dry roast some flat bread, which fed them both for the night.

Some evenings, sitting on a wooden bed in the corner of that large room, the postmaster would start talking about the people back home—his younger brother, mother and his elder sister, the ones whose thoughts filled him with pain in his loneliness. These were things he thought about constantly but could not express to the workers at the indigo factory; yet it never seemed implausible talking about them with an uneducated young girl. Eventually it came to pass that the girl would refer to his family as Ma, Didi, Dada as though she had known them forever. She even had a picture of them in her heart, as she imagined them to be.

Once during the rainy season, a warm, gentle breeze was blowing in the cloudless midday sky, and as though the languid earth was exhaling, a certain perfume rose from the damp grass and trees basking in the sun, while an adamant bird voiced its monotonous complaint before Nature in a very melancholic tune.

Our postmaster had nothing to do—the shimmering movement of rain bathed young leaves against the sun brightened clusters of cloud and all that remained of the recent rains was truly something to look at., As he looked at them he thought, 'if only I had someone now who would be mine alone—a loving human playmate of the heart'. Gradually, it seemed that the bird was voicing the very same thing and so were the murmuring leaves of that lonely, shaded afternoon. No one would know or even believe it but this was the feeling that came over the lowly postmaster of that little hamlet on those silent afternoons of the long days of rest.

He sighed and called out, 'Ratan?'

She had been sitting under the guava trees happily eating the fruits, but she came quickly when she heard his call, and upon arrival, breathlessly asked, 'Brother, were you calling me?'

'I want to teach you how to read,' he said and after starting off with the basic alphabet, he moved on to conjugated letters within a few days.

There was no respite to the rains of Shravan. All over, the ponds and canals were deluged and all day long the only sounds that could be heard were those of rain and frog song. The village roads were almost impassable and people had to take boats when going to the market.

One such day the rain had taken up from very early in the morning. Though the student had been waiting for a very long time by sitting patiently near the door, the usual call had not arrived and finally seeing no point in waiting outside, she decided to walk in with her books. Upon entering she saw that he was lying down and assumed he was resting; as she was about to leave the room in silence he suddenly called out her name.

She quickly turned and asked, 'Were you sleeping?'

The postmaster faintly replied, 'I do not feel too well—would you feel my forehead for me?'

When sick and alone in a foreign place on a rainy day such as this, one yearns for a bit of tender attention. The memories of a mother's soft palm, placed on a warm brow come to mind. The mind wants to believe that there is a gentle affectionate feminine presence—perhaps a mother or a sister seated next to the sickbed—when one is all alone abroad. In this case the wish did not go unfulfilled. Ratan was no longer just a girl. She immediately took on the mantle of a mother and called the doctor, gave him his medication at the right times and stayed awake all night, preparing foods suitable for convalescence and asking him a hundred times, 'Dear brother, are you feeling just a little better?'

After many days, the postmaster rising weakly from his sickbed decided that he had had enough and that he would just have to get a transfer from the place. After writing of the unhealthy conditions, he applied for a transfer with the head office in Kolkata.

When she was freed from the duties of nursing, Ratan could once again take her old place outside the door. However, she was no longer summoned as in the days gone past; occasionally she would peer inside and see the postmaster either sitting down with an extremely absent look on his face or lying on his string bed. While Ratan waited to be called, he waited eagerly for news of his transfer. She went over her old lessons a thousand times as she waited outside the door. She fretted that there would come a day when she might suddenly be called in and she would surely make a mistake with her conjugated letters. Finally one evening, after about a week, she was called.

She anxiously came in and asked, 'Were you calling me?'

He replied, 'Ratan, I am going tomorrow.'

'Where are you going, sir?'

'Home.'

'When will you be back?'

'Never again!'

Ratan did not ask another question. The postmaster told her how he had applied for a transfer but it had been refused. He had therefore resigned and was going back home. Not a word was said for a long time, as the lamp continued to flicker and water dripped into an earthen bowl in a corner of the room from a leak in the broken roof.

After a while, she slowly got up and went to the kitchen to make the rotis for the night. She could not work as quickly as the other days; I suppose her mind was burdened with many thoughts.

After the postmaster had finished his meal, the girl asked him, 'Sir, will you take me to your home?'

The postmaster laughed and said, 'How can that be!' but he did not think it necessary to explain to the girl all the reasons why it was impossible.

The words kept coming back to her all night as she drifted in and out of sleep. *'How can that be!'*

When the postmaster woke in the morning, he saw the water for his bath was ready; he liked bathing from a bucket as per his habit from his days in Kolkata. She had been unable to ask him when he was leaving for a number of reasons but had gone to the river late at night to fetch the water so that he would have it in the morning. When he finished bathing she was called. Ratan entered the room silently and looked at his face once in silence as she waited for her master's command. He said, 'Ratan, I will tell the gentleman replacing me so that he looks after you just as I have; you will not have to worry because I am leaving.' There is no doubt that these words came from a very affectionate and compassionate heart but who can read a woman's soul? Ratan had put up with many of her employer's admonishments in silence but she could not bear this kindness at all. She suddenly sobbed out in anguish, 'No, you don't have to say anything to anyone, I do not want to stay on!'

The post master had never seen Ratan behave this way and he was plunged into silence.

The new post master arrived. The old one explained the nature of the job to him and prepared to leave. When he was ready, he called Ratan and said to her, 'I have never been able to give you anything. Today I will give you some money. This should see you through, for a few days.'

He took all the money he had received as pay, keeping back a little for expenses on the road. Ratan fell at his feet, clasping them as she said, 'Please I beg you, you do not have to give me a thing, no one needs to think about me'—and quickly escaped from there.

The former post master sighed as he carried his carpet bag and umbrella himself and entrusted his blue and white striped tin trunk to a porter, before walking slowly to the boat.

When he got on the boat and it set sail, the rain swollen river lapped against the boat like the heaving sobs of the earth and he felt a very acute pain within his heart—the saddened face of an ordinary village girl seemed to express the unsaid sorrow of the entire world. At one time he felt very intensely, 'Let me go back and bring that orphaned girl with me.' But then the sails filled with wind, the rain fed currents quickened and the village was left behind as the cremation grounds came into view. His heart realised as he floated along, that life was full of such separations and endings, what benefit was then in returning? Who on earth can we really claim as our own?

But Ratan could not think of anything philosophical. She kept wandering around that post office in a flood of silent tears. I suppose she had some faint hope of the young man coming back and that tenuous tie made it harder for her to leave. Alas, the foolish human heart! Misconceptions die hard and all logic takes much time to enter; even the greatest proofs are cast aside as false hope is embraced with both arms and gathered into the bosom beside all cost. Finally it escapes after having sucked the heart dry of all life. The scales fall away from one's eyes and the soul seeks another such trap to submit to eagerly.

(Postmaster – Golpo Guchcho)

The Girl

Bright her complexion, red coral at her throat.
I have gazed in wonder
Upon her.
With huge dark eyes
She looked unhesitatingly back
A girl in the first bloom of youth,
She was close to me in years.
I clearly remember the picture. The doors
Were open to the south
The morning sunshine bathing the tops of the nut tree
Thick green leaves looked towards the pale
blue of the sky.
A white sari draped around the young form,
Its black border falling about her feet.

Two gold bangles on two shapely arms.
The pages of a holiday afternoon
Held that image. She beckoned me often
To that place where the whims of fate draw visions
Creating illusions within the reach
Of the dreams of a young boy.
Illusion found shape
And cast an invisible shadow across my body and soul
Subtle her touch.
I could not find the courage to speak.
My soul ached to a very softly murmured tune
But she is far, she is so far away,
From where the rain tree's topmost branches are
Slowly a faint perfume alights in the depths of my heart.
One day she came with news of a doll's marriage,
To invite me.
Laughter broke easily from the others
Invited. I stood, a shy boy
At one side numbed with restraint. Evening
passed to no avail,
I cannot recall what I was served.
I watched as two swift feet came and went
A black border dancing around them.
Furtively I saw, her bangles were as poured sunshine
Trapped about her arms. Requests and pleas
In her tender voice I heard.
When I returned to my room
That echoed in my mind
The remaining half of that night.

After that one day
Our acquaintance became easy.
One day I took her name
Called her even.
One day fear disappeared,
Playful teasing accompanied the words exchanged.
Sometimes an imagined fault
Gave reason for pretended anger.
At other times cruel humour and irony
Gave cause for sorrow.
Sometimes blame
For the crime of not knowing.
Sometimes I have seen her in careless moments
She was cooking, she felt no shame.
Many a masculine confusion of mine
She viewed with intense feminine pride.
One day she said, 'I can read palms.'

Holding my hand she bent over the lines to read
Saying, 'Your nature
Lacks the ability to show love.' In reply I said nothing at all.
The real reward of touch
Cancelled the shadow of that unjust reproach.

It really never went away
The pain of incomplete knowing.
The distance to a thing of beauty is never diminished,
Closeness merely gives infinite proof of how
Far away it still is.

Day after day full of joy and sadness
Fade into the western sky.
The skies darken with beauty as time goes by,
The light of the new season
Make the fields of gold sing with a sense of departure.
A slow boat moving for the unknown laden with dreams.

(Shyama – Santiniketan, 31st October 1938)

Flower of the Night

Flower of the night is what I have named her; the
village folk say that she is dark
On a cloudy day I saw her in the fields, a dusky girl
with the eyes of a deer.
She had no veil to hide herself from view, instead
her hair streamed down her back,
Dark? She may well have been, but all I saw were
those doe eyes of deepest black.

Dense the clouds that gather darkness close as
two cows bellow in fear
The dusky one hurries on anxious feet as from her
hut she ventures far
She lifts her eyes skyward under arched brows, listening to
distant thunder roll

Dark? She may well have been, but all I saw were those
doe eyes of deepest black.

The wind rose suddenly from the east, sending waves
rippling through the ripening grain
I stood alone on the edge of that day, not another
soul upon that plain
Did she look towards me? Who can tell, only
she and I will ever know.
Dark? She may well have been, but all I saw were
those doe eyes of deepest black.

Clouds of inky black grow in the north eastern sky
Soon soft cloud shadows will descend on forests
dense with wait
Finally the skies yield rain's bountyful spate
Dark? She may well have been, but all I saw were
those doe eyes of deepest black.

Flower of the night is what I call her; let the others
say what they want
I saw her in the fields of a little village, a dusky girl
with the eyes of a deer.
She had not veiled herself in shame; she had not had
the time to do that
Dark? She may well have been, but all I saw were those doe
eyes of deepest black.

(Krishnakoli – 18th June 1900)

The Sleeping One

Like the sons of kings I have been to many lands
Seen the seven seas and thirteen rivers of lore.
Wherever there was a beautiful face to be found
I have seen till nothing was left any more.
Some might have said a few words,
Some looked away from me,
Some smiles cut me like blades of steel
Some smiles were like tears unshed.

Some went back with pride,
Some looked back in grief again and again.
Some never spoke of it to anyone,
Some have mourned in softly murmured song.
This is how I left the lands I found.

But far away, where the sky meets the land
Lies a princess alone in the Kingdom of Sleep
There, I placed my ring upon her hand.
Once upon a time in my youth
I awoke startled from a dream,
Leaving my bed I came outside and stood
Looking upon the earth as it lay before me.
The evening star was growing pale and faded
As night ceded to dawn in the skies of the east.

Each corner was waking to the day
The earth still resting in sleep's sway.
An endless path stretched ahead of me,
Trees shaded it on either side,
As I gazed upon the distant sight
A thought came to my mind.
At the end of the very same night
Upon this earth in some undiscovered land,
Glowing on some foam white bed
Somewhere a princess dreamt.

On my horse I started off at once,
Crossing many lands and beyond.
Arriving on a hazy evening
At the gates of the Kingdom of Sleep.
Everyone was steeped in slumber there.
Nowhere was there a living soul,
By the river, lulled by flowing water
Sleeps a vast city on its own.

I dreaded to take even a single step
For fear I should awake the whole populace.
I set foot in the palace with care
My fear walked one step ahead.
The king slept, alongside his queen,
The princes slept, the heir and his brother.
In one room burned a jewelled lamp,
There slumbered the princess from my dream.

The bed was like a lotus blossom
Upon that lay a slender vine of human form.
I looked at her face unblinking,
While my heart ached with a pain very like pleasure.
Clouds of dark hair hid
The pillow with wave upon wave.
One arm lay across her breast
The other had dropped away in sleep.
Her clothes were in disarray,
Like young leaves her bodice covered
A pair of untouched flowers destined for the worship of a god.
I looked upon this, words I could never find
A dream from the Land of Sleep.
A princess upon her own bed
With her own beauty alone surrounded.

I clutched my agitation to myself,
My heart beat fit to burst.
I kneeled upon the ground,
And kissed the sleeping eyes without a sound.

It was like looking through a pair of doors
To see what treasures and peace lay within
As I looked at the stars of her pupils
Through her sleep parted eyelids.
I wrote upon a bark sheet with black soot
My name and other words about me.
I wrote, 'Sleeping One,
I give my very soul to thee.'
I tied the missive with a golden thread
To the jewelled strands around her throat.
In the Land of Sleep sleeps the daughter of a king,
To her I have pledged my soul, my everything.

(Nidrita – 28th May 1892)

Everlasting Love

It is as if I have loved only you
In a hundred different forms, again and again
Through this cycle of birth, down the ages without fail.
My captivated soul has forever
Spun words into garlands of song
In many a form you have worn them,
Happily accepting my gift of love
Through this cycle of birth, down the ages without fail.
The more I hear that long lost story,
And the pangs of that ancient love,
Of a tale of love lost and found,
From distant memory comes a vision
Across the dark night of time
At last I see your face, eternally bright,

A constant guiding star in midst of life.
We have swam together
You and I, in this stream of love
From its source in the heart
Of times long gone by.
We have played with delight
With a million other lovers
Bathed in tears of happiness and pain,
Bashful in the grasp of togetherness—
A timeless bond in ever changing form.
That undying flame of love
Today finds its place
In glorious abandon at your feet.
Universal joy and sorrow,
The devotion within the universal soul,
Have all come to bear fruit in this one love of ours
Imbued with the memory of all who have loved before—
One hears it in the songs sung by the poets down the ages.

(Ananta Prem – Jorasanko, 17th August 1889)

The Ordinary Woman

I am a woman who lives far from the world
You will not have met me.
I have read your recent novel, Sharatbabu,
'Garland of Stale Flowers'.
Your heroine Elokeshi almost died
At the age of thirty-five.
She was competing with a woman of twentyfive.
I found that you are generous indeed
You allowed her to win.

Let me tell you something about myself.
I am young.
Someone came into my life
At this tender age.

This brought a thrill to my body
I briefly forgot that I am so very ordinary.
There are thousands like me
Women, touched briefly by the magic of youth.

Let me plead with you,
Please write about an ordinary woman.
Who has much to feel sorry for.
Even within that plainness,
If anything extraordinary did hide,
How is she to prove it?
Are there any of us out there, able to see it?
They only see the illusions of youth,
Their minds do not seek the truth
To them we are mirages.
Let me tell you why I brought this up
Let us say, his name is Naresh.
He professed he had never met anyone like me.
I was not brave enough to believe such a statement
Nor strong enough to see it as a lie.

One day, he went abroad.
Sometimes I got a letter or two.
I used to think, 'Good God, there are so many women there,
There must be crowds of them.
And are they all extraordinary?
Such brains, such brilliance!
And have they all discovered the one Naresh Sen
Who was hidden amongst many when he was here?'

In his latest letter he writes,
'Went bathing in the sea with Lizzie.'
He even quotes from a Bengali poem,
That part about the heavenly dancer Urvashi rising from the sea.
Then they sat side by side on the sands,
Watching the waves of the blue sea before them
And the sky above filled with spotless sunshine.
Lizzie said to him very softly,
'You have just arrived; you will leave in a short while
Two halves of a shell
Let there be a perfect, priceless teardrop in between them.'
What a lovely way of saying things!
Here Naresh has written,
'Even if they are made up words
Are they not beautiful?
A diamond encrusted golden flower is not real but
still real enough.'
You can understand
How this makes me feel.
A thorn of comparison from his letter, piercing
straight into my heart.
I am exceedingly ordinary.
I own nothing of worth,
So I cannot pay for what has value.
But I beseech you, let that be
Let me be indebted for eternity.

I implore you; please write a story Sharatbabu,
About a very ordinary woman

One who must compete from afar
With not one but maybe seven such extraordinary women
Like seven suns of womanhood.

I know, I am unfortunate,
I have already lost.
But when you write about the ordinary woman,
Let her win, on my behalf.
Let my heart swell with pride on her behalf.
May your pen be blessed.

Give her the name Malati
Which by the way, is my name.
Never fear,
There are many such Malatis in this land
All ordinary women.
They do not know French or German,
But they do know how to cry.

How will you make her win?
You are magnanimous, mighty is your pen.
Perhaps you will take her down the path of sacrifice.
To the depths of sorrow, like Shakuntala!
So please, be kind to me.

Come down to my level.
As I lie in bed in the dark of night
And ask for the impossible from my god
I know I will never get that.

But may your heroine receive all of that.
Let Naresh be in London for seven years,
Let him fail his examinations again and again,
In the midst of his circle of admiring females.
In the mean time, Malati completes her MA
From Calcutta University.

Let her come first in Mathematics with one stroke of your pen
But if you stop there,
Your fame as a literary genius would be sullied.
Whatever my condition is,
Do not rein in your imagination.
You are not a miser like my fate.

Send this woman to Europe.
There, their knowledgeable, their wise, their brave
Their poets, their artists, their kings
Let them surround her in great numbers.
Let them discover her like astronomers
Not just as a scholar, but as a woman too.
Let her world-conquering magic win them.
Let that mystery unfold, not in this ignorant nation.
In the land where there are connoisseurs, sympathizers
There are Englishmen, Germans and Frenchmen.
Let them felicitate her at gatherings,
Where famous names will gather.
Let us imagine that praise is being showered on her,
She walks amongst that, unimpressed.
A galleon in full sail upon the waves.

Everyone whispers about the beauty of her eyes
They say the clouds of India's monsoon and the brightness of her summer sun
Unite in her bewitching eyes.

(Let me say here
My eyes truly are blessed by the gods.
I had to say this myself,
I have not yet met any European aficionado.)
Let Naresh come and stand there,
Alongside, his band of extraordinary women.

And what happens after that?
Like the children's rhyme
My plant withers
As my dream comes to an end.
Alas! Ordinary woman
Alas! Such a waste of the Creator's energy!

(Shadharon Meye – 13th August 1932)

The Two Birds

The caged bird lived in a cage wrought from gold
The free bird lived in the forest.
Once upon a time how they met, I know not
The Creator was musing over what thought.
The forest bird said, 'Caged brother of mine,
Let the two of us fly to the forest deep.'

The bird of the cage said, 'You of the forest, come
Let us live in peace within familiar keep.'
The forest bird said, 'No,
I refuse to be chained.'
The bird of the cage said, 'Alas,
How will I venture out in the forest?'
The forest bird then sat and sang

All the songs of the forest that he knew.
The bird of the cage repeated the words he had learnt—
The two spoke in two separate tongues.
The forest bird said, 'Caged brother dear,
Can you not sing a song of the forest wild.'

The caged bird said, 'Wild brother of mine,
You can learn these songs of caged design.'
The forest bird said, 'Never,
I do not want songs that are by another.'
The caged bird said, 'Alas,
How can I sing about the trees so wild?'
The wild bird said,, 'The sky so blue,
No limits anywhere for me or for you.'
The caged bird said,, 'Look at this cage so neat
Covered am I on all sides.'

The wild bird urged, 'Let yourself go,
Soar among the clouds just this once.'
The caged bird replied, 'In this peaceful home
Tie yourself down for some time.'
The wild bird declared, 'No,
Where is the chance of flying within!'
The caged bird said, 'Alas,
How does one rest for a while upon the clouds?'
The two birds loved each other thus
But never found each other close.
Their beaks kissed through the bars of the cage
As their eyes spoke silent words.

They could not understand what the other said
They did not know themselves.
They beat their wings in pained isolation,
Crying, 'Come near'.
The wild bird said, 'No,
What if the door closes upon me suddenly?'
The caged bird said, 'Alas,
I have not the strength to fly to thee.'

(Dui Pakhi – Shahajadpur, July 1892)

Shubha

When the girl was named Shubhashini or she who is sweetly spoken at birth, no one could have predicted that she would be unable to speak. Her older sisters had been named Shukeshini and Shuhashini and her father was forced to comply with the demands of rhythm. Today everyone calls her Shubha for short.

Her sisters were married off after much careful searching for grooms and spending of large sums of money; but now the youngest was becoming a silent burden on the hearts of her parents.

Not everyone understands that the one who cannot speak is still able to feel. People would discuss their worries about her future in her very presence. She had come to realise from childhood that her birth was the Almighty's curse upon her father's home. This made her try and hide herself away continually from the prying eyes of others. She thought it was best if everyone forgot her. However, pain is not that easily forgotten. It lived on in her parents' hearts.

Her mother was especially conscious of Shubha's existence and saw it as one of her own failings. This is because a mother sees a daughter as more a part of her than a son is; any incompleteness in a daughter becomes a special reason for her to feel ashamed. In fact, Shubha's father Banikontho loved her just that little bit more than his other daughters but her mother believed her to be an aberration from her womb and was very harsh with her indeed.

Shubha had no words to utter, but she did have a pair of beautiful, dark eyes shaded by long lashes and her mouth trembled like a young leaf whenever emotion affected her.

The feelings that we express with words have to be constructed somewhat through our own efforts; a bit like translation, it is not always done correctly and often even wrongly due to an inability to use words. But eyes like hers do not need help in translating emotion—the mind casts its own shadows upon them. Feelings are sometimes expressed and withdrawn from them, sometimes they flash with fire and sometimes they die down, sometimes they gaze unblinking like the setting moon, while at other times they flicker like lightning. When one has never known any other language apart from that of an expressive face, the eyes have a language of their own, a language of infinite breadth and unreachable depth, much in the manner that a clear sky is the stage upon which sunrise and sunset, shadow and light play their parts. This silent girl mirrored the grand scale of solitude one sees in nature. The other children feared her and refused to play with her. She was silent and friendless like a lonely afternoon.

Their village was called Chandipur. The river that flowed nearby was one of the region's smaller rivers; like a daughter of an ordinary family, it was not in the habit of venturing very far, its tireless slender form flowing as required within its own banks, maintaining close ties with the villages on both sides. People lived on either side on the high, tree-shaded banks while the river ran along the shallow course—a guardian spirit of the villages—spreading her benevolence with joy as she went about her way, oblivious to anything else.

Banikontho's house was right on the river. The split bamboo fences, the eight-tiered roofline, the cowshed, the husking room, the haystacks, the tamarind tree, the mango and jackfruit groves and the banana orchards attracted attention from the passing river boat passengers. I do not know whether anyone spotted the mute girl in the midst of this picture of domesticated plenty, but whenever she found a moment's respite from household chores, she would come and sit upon the banks.

The splashing of the river, the daily noise of people, the boatman's song, the bird calls, and the rustling of trees—through these sounds and cries, it was as if nature was compensating for her lack of speech and speaking for her and these combined with the movements of the surroundings broke upon the shores of her forever silenced soul like the waves of the sea. These varied sounds of nature and the varied movements; these too were the language of the mute, a universal expression of the language of Shubha's long-lashed eyes and they carried signals, gestures, songs, tears and sighs, from the minute insects that sang in the grass to the far away stars.

At midday when the boatmen left for lunch, the villagers rested indoors, the birds called no more and the boats stopped plying, the world put a sudden halt to its activity and became very quiet and underneath that vast angry firmament only two things sat facing one another—mute nature in broad sunshine and an unspeaking girl in the little shade cast by a tree.

It was not as if Shubha did not have a small group of close friends. The family's two cows Sarvashi and Panguli had never heard their own names on her lips but they knew her footsteps—she had a wordless keening they understood better than words. They knew better than the humans when she was cosseting them, when she was scolding them and when she was cajoling them.

Shubha would enter the cow shed and cradle Sarvashi's neck in her arms as she rubbed her cheek near her ear, while Panguli gazed at her gently and licked her. She visited them three times a day as a rule; and also a number of times outside that. On the days that she was at the receiving end of harsh words at home, she would come to her mute friends unannounced—her patient sorrowful look would be accepted with a blind understanding of her inner anguish and they would come close to her and gently rub her arms with their horns, trying to console her with their wordless eagerness.

There were goats and kittens apart from these two but Shubha's friendship with them was not on such an equal footing. Nonetheless they showed sufficient faithfulness to her. The kitten would happily occupy Shubha's warm lap, both during day and at night and prepare to doze, indicating that the movements of her soft fingers along its neck and back were especially conducive to inviting sleep.

Among the more advanced creatures Shubha had found a companion, but it was hard to judge what their relationship was, as this was a living thing with language. In this they were not equal.

This was the young son of the Goshain family—his name was Pratap. He was completely idle. After much effort, his parents had given up on any hopes of seeing him ever finding work and doing something useful for the family. Lazy people have one advantage; even though their family may get annoyed with them, they will be loved by unrelated people—not having much to do makes them public property. Just like towns should have one or two non-residential government run gardens, villages should have a couple of spare idle souls who belong to the public. Whenever there is a shortage of hands at completing a job or mounting a play, these people can come in handy.

Pratap's main hobby was catching fish with a rod. One can quite easily while hours away in this fashion. He was often seen in the afternoons engaged in this pursuit on the river's edge. He often met Shubha while he was there. No matter what he did, Pratap was happier with a companion. A wordless companion is the best thing during fishing—which was why Pratap understood Shubha's worth. This is why, while everyone else called her Shubha, Pratap called her Shu with a bit of extra affection.

Shubha used to sit under the tamarind tree and Pratap would stand a short distance away watching the water where he had cast his line. He was allowed to chew on one betel leaf and she used to prepare this and bring it for him. As she sat there watching him, she often wondered whether she could be of some help to him in some little way and thus indicate to him that she too was not entirely unimportant. But there was nothing to do. She would then ask for supernatural powers from her Creator to be able to do something so amazing that Pratap would be astounded enough to say, 'Really, I never knew our Shubhi had such abilities.'

Let us imagine Shubha was a water nymph;—she would slowly emerge from the river and leave a jewel from the very hood of a snake upon the stone of the bathing platform; Pratap would then leave his fishing alone and dive into the depths with that treasure to reach the underworld, where he would see a silver palace. In that palace, on a bed of gold, who should be sitting but our Shubha, that mute girl from Banikontho's family—our Shu, the only princess of that glittering silent nether palace of the deep! Could that not ever happen? Was it so impossible? In reality nothing is impossible, but Shu was still a daughter to her father's family rather than to that unpopulated kingdom under the water and she was completely unable to do something to amaze Pratap, the son of the Goshain family.

Shubha was gradually growing up and was slowly starting to feel her own presence. It had been as if on a certain full moon-lit night, a tide from some sea had come into her soul and filled it with a new indescribable spirit of self awareness. She would look at herself, think and question herself but fail to arrive at the answers.

Late on some full moon nights she would open the doors to her bedroom and timidly look outside to see that the moon drenched nature all around her was also awake and waiting while the world slept—transported by the mysterious blush of youth to thrill and sorrow, to the final limits of endless solitude and even beyond that, where it pulsated ceaselessly, unable to form a single word. She was a silent restless girl who was waiting, at the periphery of silent yet restless nature.

Her parents were worried about the presence of an unmarried daughter at home. People had started to criticise them. It was even rumoured that they were soon to be ostracised over the issue. The fact that Banikontho was financially comfortable and able to eat fish with his rice both morning and night, had made him some enemies.

The husband and wife discussed the matter at great length and one day Bani left the village. He would be going away for a few days.

Finally one day he came back and announced to his family, 'Let us go to Kolkata.'

So, preparations started to take place. Shubha's entire soul grew heavy, drenched with sorrow like a mist covered dawn. An uncertain apprehension made her stay close to her parents continually for a few days like a voiceless animal—her beautiful eyes trying to read something from their faces, but they did not explain what was going to happen to her.

One day Pratap smiled at her as he cast his line and said, 'Hey Shu, I hear a husband has been found, and that you are going to get married? Don't forget us.' And he went back to fishing.

Shubha looked at Pratap, her eyes like those of a wounded deer that looks at the hunter in silence, questioningly as if saying *what did I do to you?* She did not sit under the tree that day, going instead to where Banikontho was smoking his hookah after his nap and sat at his feet crying silently as she looked into his eyes. Soon, tears rolled down his aging face as he tried to console her.

They were to go to Kolkata the next day. Shubha went to the cowshed to bid farewell to the companions of her childhood. She fed them with her own hands and embraced them, while gazing at them, as her eyes spoke volumes and tears dripped from her eyelashes.

It was the twelfth night after the full moon (*Shukladwadoshi*). Shubha came out of her bedroom and lay prostrate on the familiar grassy bed of the river bank—as if she was trying to cling to this vast mute mother earth saying, 'Do not let me go, please hold me with your arms too.'

Shubha's mother dressed her with great care one day, in the Kolkata house. She managed to cover up her natural appeal with a lot of jewellery and tamed her hair with ribbons of silk. Shubha wept profusely throughout, and all the while, her mother said many sharp words regarding the puffy eyes that were likely to result from this but her tears were unabated.

The groom himself came to see her along with his friends—her parents were worried, fearful and anxious, as if the deity had himself arrived to select the sacrificial beast. Her mother spoke to her with such venom that she was moved to twice as many tears when she finally was presented for inspection.

The examiner said after a long inspection, 'Not bad.'

He was especially influenced by the girl's tears, concluding that she had a good heart and deciding that if that heart was this pained at the prospect of separation from her parents, it would dote on him as well when in time it was his. Like pearls from an oyster, the girl's tears only increased her value yet they did not speak for her.

A very auspicious date was decided upon for the marriage.

The parents went back to Chandipur after giving their mute daughter away to a complete stranger—their honour and fortunes in the hereafter were safe once again.

Shubha's husband was working in the west and he took his wife with him when he left, shortly after the marriage.

Within a couple of weeks everyone understood that the new bride was mute. What no one understood was that it was not her fault. She had not tricked any one. Her eyes had said everything but no one had understood. She would look around—she had no words to express herself, seeing that the known faces that would have understood her silent language were not there—a great unspoken lament rose in her eternally silenced heart—and no one but her abandoned fate heard that.

The next time he selected a wife, her husband used both eyes and ears to judge so that he could marry a girl who was able to speak.

(Shubha – Golpo Guchcho)

The Invitation

I remember, it seems I once wrote
Dearest or beloved, to you on a note.
I suppose, today they only write a name—
Let that be, nameless you remain the same.
You demand poetry from me and my pen
Words that rhyme in complex refrain
At your door my words seek much less
A quiver of kohl, gentle eyes! Largesse!
It is perhaps best to keep my words simple
Answer my call at the slightest ruse you can find
When the time is over, return to your space
But till then, let us linger face to face.
Your sari encircles your bare feet
It's purple, the colour of Phalsa berries so sweet
Place it as a veil upon your hair so sleek
Dark border glowing against your cheek.

A stray curl of hair trembling in the breeze
Let them play about that forehead as they please
A magnolia blossom behind your right ear
Comes to life as your neck moves in answer.
The jasmine buds in the afternoon you wore
Open up as your heat warms them in the evening hour.
From afar your secret fragrance will alert
The news of your arrival within my eager heart
Let me remind you of just one thing here
That pair of little rubies I gifted once
Like tears of blood frozen just for you to wear
How many times have you forgotten they are there?
Another wish comes unbidden to my mind,
I know it does not suit rhyme of this kind.
To sing of it I know is completely wrong,
Unimportant it could well be but still the desire is strong.
These days one can hardly expect golden lamps alight
Let alone the music of a golden beena in full flight.
Just perhaps a silken cloth upon a woven basket,
A few sun hued mangoes will provide equal delight.

Add some other cooked dishes to make a good meal
Finding rhymes would test me a great deal.
Still, they are much loved, I add in haste
As you must know, desire lives most happily with taste.
Look, there is that wretched modern spirit,
Makes me inevitably lose my wit,
I know of no heavenly nymph misguided
That brings delight to my palate jaded.

Still there is little harm in stating this clearly,
The secrets of my innermost soul,
A stomach content and satisfied
Is friend to a happy heart and mind.
Sweetmeats made by a pretty pair of hands,
Fish, meat and rice and other viands.
When they appear spiced with love and care,
Surely there can be nothing that is better!
I imagine, your eyes flashing with quick humour,
As you think, a gentle smile playing upon that mouth,
All these are simply a well disguised endeavor
To present as poetic hints my demands uncouth.
Fine, laugh then at my obvious greed
Be reserved with granting your favours.
If you come empty handed, that too will fill my need.

Those two hands are also precious indeed.
That is best then, you come just by yourself,
Let the breeze carry a trace of your scent,
We will meet, just the two in that hour silent.
The evening star watches perched on the Shirish boughs.
If you do have to leave afterwards
Leave your jasmine garland behind
Yaman will play to the beat within my heart
Afterwards the poet will have to get to work.

The more I write, thoughts rise unbidden
Whose name do I pen on the envelope today?
I sigh deeply over the thought as I ruminate,

Where did this all start, on what long gone date?
A picture comes to mind, the hour was of sparkling light
You had just had an early bath
Your face a picture of innocence, you were only sixteen
Your body wrapped in a sari of striped design.

A dot of kumkum shines where the brows meet,
White oleander blossoms at the ear,
I have seen that soft swan like neck
Desirable with silken tresses draped on it.
A thick garland coiled on a copper plate,
Covered with a damp cloth for freshness.
You have laid a mat out in the shade
Why do you think that I do not know.
Today that same poet writes this letter
Evening shade paints the shadowed room darker
The wall a screen for the memories of that day
Not a sound except for the ticking of time itself.
There lies your old book of lists
In the drawer, an unused coin or two.
How many days has it been since, I dare not think,
All I can do is write this letter of invitation.
Memories come of you sitting at the eastern window
Balls of yarn warm upon your lap,
Eager eyes expecting someone to appear
Your anchal trails forgotten on the floor.

Sunlight slants on half the roof
The rest of it in soothing shade

The pots lined by the wall yield
The sweet scent of murraya up to the wind.
This letter does not need a hurried reply
I might as well place it back in the drawer.
Come if you can upon silent feet
Clasp my eyes shut suddenly from behind.
Spread the perfume of your tresses in the sky
Bring the timid tinkle of your bracelets,
Bring sweet dream-laden night,
And days filled with indolent delight.
You and I meeting in intimate isolation
Stilled in joy, silent sweetness overflowing
Blissful hours pass as I look upon you
Your palms held within mine.

(Nimantran – Chandannagore, June 14th 1935)

The Flute

In Milkman Kinu's lane
There is a double storeyed house where
Iron grilles bar a ground floor room
From the street right next to it.

Salt draws maps across the walls
Damp patches them with seas.
A cheap cloth print
Of Ganesh who grants wishes
Stuck to the door.

There is another creature that lives here
At the same rent.
A gecko.
The only difference between us
He rarely knows hunger.

At twenty five rupees
As junior clerk at a merchant office.
The Dutta family feeds me
After I tutor their son.

I walk around Sealdah station
Each evening and save
On electricity at home.

Engines chug in
The whistle marks time
Passengers rush like ants
The porters roar in self importance
And then it is half past ten
I return to lonely quiet darkness.

My aunt lives in a little village on the Dholeswari River.
The girl her niece by marriage
An alliance had been fixed with this wretch.
The hour was good, everything set
I escaped without a word.
At least the girl was saved
I carried on as I was.

She did not come into my life, but daily into my mind
A *dhakai* sari, forehead touched with a red dot.

Dense rain shrouds the day.
Trams cost money
Lateness eats into the pay.

The alley gives birth to
Little heaps, mango peel and stone, jackfruit pith
Fish gills.
Dead kittens
Ashes to ashes, dust and much more.

My umbrella like a much docked salary slip
A patchwork of missing pieces.
My office clothes
Like a mind in the grip of religion
Always drenched in pity.

The dark shadows of monsoon
Enter the damp room
And collapse comatose
Like trapped animals.

Day and night I feel I have
Tied my lot with the half dead world.

Nearby lives Kantobabu,
Long hair, combed back carefully
Expressive eyes
Refined his tastes.
He plays the cornet.

Sometimes a tune wakes up
In the cloying horror of the air of the lane
Sometimes late at night

Or by the half light of dawn
Sometimes in the afternoon
When sparkling light plays with shadows.

Suddenly in the evening
Strains of Sindhu Barwa rise
The whole sky sings
About that timeless pain of separation.

At that very moment it is clear that
This lane is but another lie in the fabric of untruths.
Like the unbearable rantings of a drunkard.

Suddenly I realise
There is little to separate Emperor Akbar
From a mere clerk.
The mournful flute
Makes both crave the divine
Leaving both torn umbrella, and regal canopy behind.

Where this song rings true
In the eternal twilight hour
There
The Dholeswari flows
Tree shade smudges the banks
The one who waits, wears
A *dhakai* sari, forehead touched with a red dot.

(Bnashi – 9th July 1932)

The Kiss

Apurbakrishna was coming home from Kolkata after acquiring his BA degree.

The river was tiny and it invariably dried up at the end of the rainy season. At the end of the month of Shravan however, it was flowing close enough to the bamboo groves and boundary fences of the village to be able to kiss their feet. After many days of rain, the sun was shining from a cloudless sky.

If we could look inside Apurba's mind as he sat in the boat, we would have seen a similar stream of thoughts glimmering in the sun, gently rippled by the breeze as he surveyed his surroundings.

The boat eventually moored at the ghat. The corner of Apurba's family home was visible through the foliage of the riverside trees. There was no one to receive him at the landing as no one knew of his arrival. As the boatman prepared to help him with his luggage, Apurba waved him away and happily descended with some alacrity, bag in hand.

As he did so, he slipped in the glutinous mud of the river bank and fell. No sooner than that happened, a sweet liquid laugh tinkled out in peals loud enough to startle the birds in the nearby peepal tree.

Apurba was extremely ashamed of what had just happened and looked around as he checked himself. He saw a girl perched on a pile of bricks freshly unloaded from the supplier's boat on to the river bank, who was laughing so hard she looked as though she might break into a hundred pieces.

Apurba recognised her as Mrinmoyee, the daughter of their new neighbours Ishan Majumdar and his wife Sharat. The family had been living on the banks of a major river some distance away and had moved to his village about two or three years ago when floods ate away at their home.

A lot of stories were told about her exploits. The men spoke about her as 'the mad girl' with affection but the mothers in the village were constantly worried and fearful about her wilful ways. All the boys were her friends, as she viewed girls of her own age with a great deal of scorn. In the world of the village children, she was a constant threat to peace.

Her father's indulgence and love had made her such a terror. Her mother never failed to complain about him over this issue when amongst friends, yet he loved his daughter so much and her tears caused him such anguish that thoughts of her absent husband made her mother incapable of disciplining her.

Mrinmoyee was a dusky skinned girl. Her short curly hair tumbled down to her back. Her expression was like that of an innocent boy. Her huge dark eyes held no shame or fear or guile. She was tall, healthy and strong-limbed and yet no one ever thought about how old she was; if they had done that, people would surely have criticised her parents for neglecting their duty in getting her married. On the rare occasions that the zamindar's boat came to the village, the villagers grew frantic with awe and the normally vocal women drew their veils half way down their faces. Mrinmoyee, however, would appear, balancing a naked infant on her hips, curly hair swinging down her back, undisturbed by the appearance of the new dignitary. She would observe everything with the fearless curiosity of a faun from a land without hunters or danger. Eventually she would return to her loyal band of boys and describe the behaviour of this new arrival in great detail.

Apurba had visited his home during holidays and seen this free-spirited child woman a few times before. He had thought about her during moments of leisure and even while busy. One sees many faces but one or two faces touch us deep inside without any prior warning. This is not just because of their beauty. There is something else; possibly that quality might be transparency. Most faces do not allow the inner human nature to be fully expressed; but the face that does allow that secret inner inhabitant to freely play across its features catches the eye instantly and becomes imprinted upon the mind. This girl's eyes and face showed glimpses of the free spirited uncontrollable woman within roaming unrestrained, like a wild deer, which was why once seen, it was difficult to forget this lively face.

Needless to say, no matter how sweet Mrinmoyee's amused laughter was, it did cause the unfortunate Apurba some pain. He quickly gave his bag to the boatman and walked in the direction of his home with a red face.

The scene had been set wonderfully. The banks of the river, the shade of trees, the song of birds, the morning sun and a twenty-year-old youth; of course the pile of bricks was not very suitable, but the one sitting on them had managed to bring a pleasant softness to even this hard seat. It was tragic that the very first foot step should reduce all poetry to a farce; such is the tyranny of fate!

Apurba walked home under the shade of trees, his clothes and bag covered in mud, while peals of laughter followed him from the brickpile.

His widowed mother was delighted at the sudden arrival of her son. People were sent off in all directions to buy milk, sweets and good fish. Even the neighbours were excited by his presence.

After the meal, Apurba's mother raised the question of his marriage. Apurba had been prepared for this. The reason was that the question had been raised much before but Apurba had insisted as a modern man, on not getting married before finishing his BA degree. His mother had waited for all this time, today she was not going to listen to any more excuses. He said, 'Let a bride be found first, we can decide on getting married afterwards.' His mother said, 'A bride has been found, you do not have to worry about that.' Apurba had also been prepared for this and said, 'I cannot get married without seeing the bride.' His mother thought she had never heard of anything so outrageous, but she still agreed.

That night when Apurba had turned his lamp off and lain down, a delightful high pitched laugh kept ringing in his ear in spite of all the other sounds of the rainy night and the silence in between. His mind kept telling him that he had to rectify that morning's fall somehow. The girl did not appreciate that he had attained much knowledge and had lived in the great city of Kolkata for a long time. Just because he had fallen in the mud did not mean he was like the other ridiculous country yokels and only fit for her disdain.

The next day Apurba was to see the prospective bride. It was not very far from his house. He dressed with some care. Putting the usual dhoti and wrap aside, he put on pyjamas and a long shirt, a turban on his head and a pair of varnished shoes on his feet before unfurling a silk parasol and setting out in the morning.

As soon as he stepped inside his prospective in-laws home, a great fuss was made over greeting him. Eventually the trembling girl was dusted, polished and coloured, wrapped with silken ribbons and encased in a delicate sari, before she was brought before him. She sat in one corner quietly with her shy head almost touching her knees and an elderly retainer sat behind her, presumably to give her courage. One of her brothers scrutinised this uninvited gatecrasher to their family with great attention, specially his turban, his watch chain and his newly-emerging beard. Apurba stroked his moustache and finally said with some gravity, 'What do you study?' No answer was forthcoming from the decorated heap of shy girlhood. After asking the same question a couple of times and a number of vicious nudges from the elderly maid from behind, the girl said very rapidly, 'Charupath Part 2, Grammar Part 1, Geography, Arithmetic and The History of India', in a low voice, without pausing for breath.

At this time a sudden sound of rapid footsteps were heard outside and within seconds Mrinmoyee rushed into the room, hair down her back, panting with her exertions. She did not look at Apurbakrishna at all but grabbed the bride's brother Rakhal's hand and started pulling him up. Rakhal was then busy exercising his abilities of observation and he refused to budge. The maid rebuked Mrinmoyee severely, but in a low voice befitting the occasion. Apurba sat like a monument to solemnity and self-respect, his turbaned head held high as he fiddled with his watch chain. Eventually, after failing to stir her friend, Mrinmoyee decided to deliver a resounding slap on his back and pull down the would be bride's veil before she stormed out of the room.

The maid kept up a low grumbling and Rakhal laughed out at the sudden unveiling of his sister. He did not think ill of the stinging slap he had received as this sort of exchange happened all the time between them. In fact, previously Mrinmoyee's hair had come half way down her back; Rakhal was the one who had suddenly cut her plait off with a pair of scissors. Enraged, she had then snatched the scissors from him and mercilessly chopped off what was left at the back till her curls lay on the ground like clusters of black grapes severed from the vine. This sort of discipline was quite the norm with them.

The silent examination session did not last for much longer. The girl somehow transformed herself from a mound to an upright figure and went indoors with the maid. Apurba was about to leave, twirling his faint moustache, when he found that his new varnished shoes were not where he had left them. Even after much looking, they remained missing.

Everyone in the house was very embarrassed and many threats and curses were muttered against the one responsible for the deed. When the shoes failed to turn up after searching, Apurba had to don a pair of old ill-fitting slippers belonging to the master of the house and carefully walk home on the muddy village path, still resplendent in his pants, his long shirt and his turban.

On the empty path by the pond he heard those peals of loud laughter again. As if a fun-loving forest nymph was suddenly overcome as she saw the outfit and the mismatched shoes.

Apurba stopped and boldly looked around. Suddenly the shameless wrongdoer appeared from the dense foliage and quickly put his lost shoes down in front of him and turned to escape upon which Apurba quickly caught her in his arms.

Mrinmoyee tried to wriggle out of his embrace, but she could not. The slanting rays of the sun came out of hiding from behind the branches and fell on her mischievous, round smiling face framed by curls. Like a curious traveller peering into the clear sunlit depths of a fast stream, Apurba looked with solemn eyes on her upturned face, into her lightning fast eyes and with an air of having left something incomplete, very slowly released his captive. If he had angrily admonished her, she would not have been amazed, but she did not understand this unusual silent punishment on this lonely path.

Her vivacious laugh filled the air like anklets tinkling at the feet of Nature and a thoughtful Apurba came home taking extremely slow footsteps.

Apurba found a number of excuses to avoid going inside the house to see his mother the whole day. He had an invitation where he went and had his meal.

It is hard to understand why a successful thinking man like Apurba was so eager to give a more complete picture of his own greatness or was so keen to restore his lost pride in the eyes of an ordinary village girl. What if a mischievous village girl thought he was ordinary? Why did it matter, if after having made him a laughing stock, she completely ignored him and wished for nothing more than to play with an ignorant, uneducated child called Rakhal. Why did he need to prove to her that he wrote book reviews for the monthly magazine *Vishwadeep* and that in his trunk, alongside perfume, shoes, Rubini's camphor, coloured writing paper and a book on playing the harmonium sat an exercise book filled with writing, waiting to make an appearance like the dawn that hides within darkness. But it is hard to convince one's own mind and Apurbakrishna Ray Esq BA was most unwilling to admit defeat to this lively village girl.

In the evening, his mother asked him when he went to the inner house, 'Apu, how did the viewing go? Did you like her?'

Apurba said rather boldly, 'The viewing went well, I liked one of them.'

'How many girls did you see?' his mother asked in amazement.

Finally, after much hesitation, it was revealed that Apurba had selected the neighbour Sharat's daughter, Mrinmoyee. What benefit then of so much education! His mother thought.

At first Apurba was very shy, but as his mother resisted the idea so strongly, he began to feel less reticent about it. He declared that he would not marry anyone at all if he could not marry Mrinmoyee. The more he thought about the placid, rather inanimate girl he had gone to see, the more he felt a sense of utter distaste about the process of marriage.

After a couple of days of sulking, refusing to eat and lack of sleep on both sides, Apurba ended up getting his way. His mother convinced herself that Mrinmoyee was still young and her mother was obviously incapable of raising a daughter well and she would soon be straightened out as soon as she came into her tutelage. Gradually she even came to think of Mrinmoyee's face as beautiful. But then immediately the vision of that short cropped hair came to mind and her heart filled with despair. She told herself that by doing her hair up tightly and applying large quantities of hair oil, this too might be fixed.

The neighbours all described this choice of Apurba's as an 'Apurba' or excellent choice. A number of them did love the incorrigible girl, but no one would have thought of her as a suitable daughter-in-law.

Word was sent to Ishan Majumdar, Mrinmoyee's father. He worked as a clerk in a station many miles away upriver, out of a tiny tin-roofed shack where he weighed luggage and sold tickets all day.

His eyes filled with tears at the thought of his beloved Mrinmoyee's wedding. It is hard to tell how much of that was due to sadness and how much was caused by happiness.

He applied for leave to his superior at the main office, giving his daughter's impending marriage as a reason. The officer declined this on grounds of insufficient need. He then wrote home asking whether the nuptials could be shifted to a week during the Pujas, but this time, Apurba's mother declined his appeal, saying there were suitable days in the current month and she saw no reason for postponing the event any way.

While both his wishes went unfulfilled, the older women decided it was their duty to tutor Mrinmoyee all day, in the responsibilities of married life. By declaring playing, running about, laughing loudly, talking to boys and eating when she felt hungry completely banned, they soon succeeded rather too well in presenting the married state as a complete nightmare. Mrinmoyee felt anxious and frightened as though she had been sentenced to a life term at the end of which the hangman's noose waited for her.

She shook her head like a wild pony and said, 'I will not get married.'

But she still did have to.

Thus began the process of educating her. Within one night Mrinmoyee's entire world came under Apurba's mother's control.

The mother-in-law started the process of correction. 'You are no child, so remember that your previous shameless habits will have to go!' she declared, extremely stony faced.

Mrinmoyee did not take the words to mean what the older woman had indicated. She thought that if it was not allowed in this house she must then go elsewhere. In the evening she was nowhere to be found. People looked all over. Eventually the traitorous Rakhal led the search party to where she was hiding. She was sitting inside a broken cart belonging to a previous festival at the local temple.

The readers will easily be able to imagine how her mother-in-law, her mother and all the local well-wishers rebuked and shamed her after this event.

At night the skies grew clouded and it began to rain. Apurba edged slowly towards Mrinmoyee on the bed and said softly into her ear,

'Mrinmoyee, do you not love me?'

Mrinmoyee said forcefully, 'No, I will never love you.' She aimed all her anger and outrage at the unjust treatment she had received at Apurba, like a lightning bolt.

'What have I done to you?' Apurba said, hurt. Mrinmoyee answered, 'Why did you have to marry me?'

There is not much one can do to give a satisfactory answer to this accusation; Apurba still said to himself that he would try everything to tame this obstinate heart.

The next day, her mother-in-law saw early warning signs of rebelliousness and locked her in her room. She fluttered like a newly caged bird inside the room for a long time. Finally, after failing to find a way out, she ripped the bed sheet to shreds with her teeth in frustration and lay on the ground weeping, calling for her father quietly.

Someone came, sat by her and affectionately tried to push her hair out of the dust and off her face. Mrinmoyee shook her head violently and moved the hand away. Apurba bent down and whispered, 'I have opened the door secretly. Come; let us go away to the back garden.' Mrinmoyi kept shaking her head and said, 'No!' Apurba tried to raise her face, holding her chin up, saying, 'Look at who is here.' Rakhal stood near the door, astounded at the sight of his friend on the floor. Mrinmoyee pushed Apurba's hand away without looking up. Apurba said, 'Rakhal is here to play with you, will you play?' Mrinmoyee said in an annoyed tone, 'No!' Rakhal too understood that something was not quite right and escaped with a sense of relief. Apurba sat there quietly. When Mrinmoyee had cried herself to sleep, he tiptoed out and locked the door behind himself.

The next day she received a letter from her father. He had sent his heartfelt blessings to the young couple as he had been unable to be present for the marriage of his daughter who was truly dearer to him than life itself.

Mrinmoyee went to her mother-in-law and said, 'I will go and visit my father.' Her mother-in-law scolded her for the sheer audacity of this sudden request, saying, 'God knows where her father lives, what an idea! Ridiculous whims!' Without saying a thing she went away. Back in her own room, Mrinmoyee shut the door and like the prayers of a completely devastated person, she started to say over and over again, 'Father, please take me away. I have no one here. I will not live much longer if I have to stay here.'

Late at night when her husband fell asleep, Mrinmoyee stealthily opened the door and left the house. Even though the clouds obscured the moon at times, there was still enough moonlight to see the path. Mrinmoyee knew nothing of the way she would have to take to her father's place of work. She had a steadfast belief that the way to anywhere in the world lay on the path the postmen took while delivering mail. She walked along that road. As she walked she grew weary and the night came to an end. When a bird or two called out tentatively in the forest without being sure of what time it was, Mrinmoyee arrived at a large market on the banks of a river. As she stood, wondering which direction to take, she heard a familiar ringing sound. The post man was coming fast with a bag of letters on his shoulder. Mrinmoyee quickly asked him, 'I want to go to Kushiganj where my father lives. Will you take me with you?' But he answered, 'I do not know where that is,' and boarded a waiting boat after rousing the boatman from his sleep. He did not have the time to be kind or ask her any questions.

Gradually the market woke up. She asked a boatman, 'Will you take me to Kushiganj?'

Before he could answer, someone from a neighbouring boat called out, 'Are you not Minu? What are you doing here?' Mrinmoyee eagerly answered, 'Bonomali! I want to go to Kushiganj to see father, take me in your boat.' Bonomali was from her village and knew just what this undisciplined girl was like. He said, 'To see your father? That is a great plan, I will take you.' Mrinmoyee happily climbed on board.

The boatman set the boat sailing. It started pouring as rain clouds hid the sky. The swollen river made the boat sway to and fro and soon Mrinmoyi was enveloped in sleep. She spread the end of her sari under the shelter and slept soundly like Nature's own child, lulled to sleep by the movement of the river.

When she woke, she found herself lying in bed at home. Seeing she had woken up, the maid left on watch started to scold her. Her mother-in-law came on hearing the maid's voice and started stating her opinions very harshly indeed. Mrinmoyee stared at her with her huge eyes. Eventually when she started blaming her father's leniency, Mrinmoyee quickly went next door and locked herself within.

Against his best judgement, even Apurba came and said to his mother, 'Ma, what is the harm in sending your daughter-in-law to her father's house for a couple of days?'

She furiously scolded Apurba on hearing this and rued the fact that even though there were so many girls across the land, he had thought it fit to bring such an irritating ill-mannered girl home as his wife.

That day, this storm of recriminations matched perfectly with the foul weather outside.

The next day, very late at night, Apurba woke Mrinmoyee very gently and said, 'Do you want to go to your father?'

Mrinmoyee grasped his hand, suddenly alert and said, 'I do.'

Apurba whispered, 'Let us go then together. I have kept a boat waiting on the river's edge.'

Mrinmoyee looked at her husband once with a very grateful look in her eyes. She then got up and changed her clothes, ready to leave. Apurba left a letter for his mother so that she would not worry and then they were off.

In the darkness of that night, on the silent empty village path Mrinmoyee held her husband's hand for the first time willingly, and with complete trust, the happiness in her heart flowed through her soft touch into her husband's veins.

The boat set off that night. Even though she was excited and happy, Mrinmoyee fell asleep very soon. The next day was filled with such freedom and happiness. There were so many villages, markets, fields and forests to look at, on either side of the river. There were so many boats plying the currents. She asked her husband a thousand questions about every little thing. What is on that boat, where have they come from, what is this place called, these and a hundred other questions that Apurba had never seen answered in any of his college texts and had never experienced during his life in Kolkata. As friends, I know you will be ashamed that he answered each of these and mostly incorrectly; calling the cargo on one boat sesame seed when he should have said linseed, calling Panchberia Ramnagar and describing the court house as the landlord's house without any hesitation. Amazingly, these incorrect answers did not hamper the enjoyment of the one who had asked the questions in complete faith.

The next evening the boat reached Kushiganj. Inside his tin shed, Ishanchandra was perched on a stool, bare-bodied in the heat, as he did his calculations in a huge leather bound ledger placed on a tiny desk by the light of a square oil lantern with sooty glass. The new couple entered and Mrinmoyee said, 'Baba!' Never had that space heard such a voice!

He started weeping. He could not decide what to say or to do. His son-in-law and daughter were like the crown prince and princess of the empire and he could not for the life of him understand how he would build them a throne out of the bags of jute in the room.

Then there was the matter of the food. He cooked his own meager meals—how would that do for such a happy day, what would he do, how would he feed them! Mrinmoyee said, 'Today we will all cook together.' Apurba showed suitable enthusiasm at this idea.

There was a lack of space, lack of helpers and a lack of food, but still, just as a fountain races out at quadrupled speed when it bursts out of a small space, their happiness flowed rich and full despite all the obstacles presented by poverty.

Three days passed like this. The steamer came twice a day; people flowed from it with noisy enthusiasm. In the evenings the riverbanks were completely empty and they were free to roam it. They prepared and made the food with much merriment over mistakes that were made through the inexperience of all three. After the food was made, it was served with much love and the tinkling of bracelets as father and husband ate together and teased Mrinmoyee about the various things she had yet to learn as a housewife and she responded to them with happy protests and pretenses of being upset. Finally, Apurba announced that it would not be wise to extend the visit any longer. Mrinmoyee begged for a few more days but Ishan said it would be better for them to go.

The day they left, he pulled his daughter close and tearfully said, 'Be happy in your new home. Let no one say that you have done anything wrong.' She left with her husband, crying as she went. Ishan returned to that small room which now felt even more joyless and resumed weighing luggage day after day, month after month.

When the errant pair came home, Apurba's mother was very solemn and said nothing to them. She did not accuse them of anything that they could defend themselves against.

This silent accusation and quiet rage hung over the entire household like a dead weight.

Eventually when it became unbearable, Apurba said, 'Ma, I have to go now, the Law classes have started.'

His mother said casually, 'What will you do with your wife?'

Apurba said, 'She will stay here.'

His mother said, 'No need for that. You can have her.' Usually she spoke in a friendlier manner. Apurba was very upset by this and said, 'Alright.'

They started preparing to go to Kolkata. One night Apurba came to bed and found Mrinmoyee crying.

He felt hurt. 'Mrinmoyee, do you not want to go to Kolkata with me?' he asked.

Mrinmoyee answered, 'No.'

Apurba asked, 'Don't you love me?' There was no answer to this. This question can have such an easy answer at times and such a complicated answer at others that it is not fair to expect an answer from a girl.

Apurba asked, 'Are you feeling sad about leaving Rakhal?'

Mrinmoyee answered easily, 'Yes.'

This young man with a BA degree felt a needle of jealousy against the child Rakhal grow within him. He said, 'I will be away for a very long time.' Mrinmoyee had nothing to say to this. 'It could be two years or more.' Mrinmoyee said, 'when you come back, bring a three-faceted Rogers knife for Rakhal.'

Apurba raised himself slightly and asked, 'So you will stay here?'

Mrinmoyee said, 'Yes, I will go and stay with my mother.'

Apurba sighed and said, 'Okay, do that. As long as you do not write to me asking me to come, I will not come. You are happy with that?'

Mrinmoyee did not see any reason to answer this and fell asleep. Apurba could not go to sleep and remained awake, propped up on the pillows.

Late at night moonlight suddenly flooded the bed. Apurba looked at Mrinmoyee in that light and felt as though someone had touched a princess with a silver wand and put her to sleep. It would now be up to him to touch her with a golden wand and wake her. She would then give him her love; the silver wand was for smiles and the golden wand was for tears.

Apurba woke her up at dawn, saying, 'It is time for me to go. Let me take you to your mother's house.'

When Mrinmoyee had stood up, Apurba held her hands and said, 'I have a request. I have helped you many times. Will you reward me for that?'

Mrinmoyee asked, amazed, 'What?'

Apurba said, 'Give me a loving kiss with all your heart.'

Mrinmoyee started laughing when she heard this strange request and saw Apurba's serious look. She controlled her laugh and looked up to kiss him—she could not get very far and dissolved in laughter. She tried this a few more times and eventually covered her face and laughed. Apurba boxed her earlobe in mock discipline.

Apurba had made a solemn promise to himself. He considered stealing kisses and gaining affection by force to be demeaning. He wanted to be rewarded like a god, with pride and voluntarily.

Mrinmoyee stopped laughing. Apurba took her by early morning light to her mother's, came back and said to his mother, 'I have thought about this and it seems that if my wife goes to Kolkata, my studies will be hampered and she too would be lonely there. As you do not want her here, I have taken her to her mother's house.'

Mother and son parted under a cloud of deeply injured feelings.

Mrinmoyee found nothing made her happy anymore at her mother's house. Everything seemed to have changed in that house. The time refused to pass. She could not decide what to do and where to go or whom to see.

Suddenly Mrinmoyee felt as though there was no one in that house or for that matter in the whole village. It was as if a solar eclipse had wiped out the light at midday. She could not understand how today she so badly wanted to go to Kolkata and yet, just the other day, this wish was furthest from her mind. She had not understood that the part of life that she had not wanted to leave behind had already become bland and tasteless to her while she had been looking the other way. She easily threw the old life away like shed leaves.

In stories one hears of master swordsmiths who can make swords so fine that they can slice a man in half without them feeling a thing. At last when shaken, they fall apart. The Creator had such a sword and Mrinmoyee had not felt him strike her at the junction between childhood and youth, yet today they fell apart as a result of upheaval and she was left to look on in pained wonder.

Her old bedchamber at her mother's house no longer seemed like hers and she wondered where had the little girl who had once lived there gone? All her memories now hummed around another house, another room, and another bed in that room.

No one ever saw Mrinmoyee outdoors any more. She could never be heard laughing. Rakhal was now afraid of her. He did not even think of playing with her.

Mrinmoyee said to her mother, 'Ma, can you take me to that house?'

Apurba's mother remembered his desolate face as he left and her heart broke. The fact that he had left his wife at her mother's in anger was very painful to her.

Suddenly one day, Mrinmoyee came and fell at her mother-in-law's feet with a sad face. The older woman immediately clasped her to her bosom. All their differences fell away. She looked at Mrinmoyee's face in amazement. The old Mrinmoyee was no longer there. This sort of sweeping change is not possible for everyone. Great change requires great will.

Her mother-in-law had planned to correct Mrinmoyee's faults one by one but an invisible force had used a quick and magical brush that had swept her clean of all flaws and had given her a new incarnation. Finally, her mother-in-law and Mrinmoyee began to understand each other and just as the branches of a tree interweave; their lives too became indistinguishable.

A calm, serene full-blown womanliness had filled Mrinmoyee's body and soul to the very brim but this gave her little pleasure. A tearful sadness clouded her heart like a rain filled cloud early in the season. This made her dark eyelashes a little more shaded; she said to herself, why did you not try to understand me even if I was too obtuse to know you? Why did you not punish me? Why did you not guide me according to your will? When I willfully refused to accompany you to Kolkata, why did you not force me to go? Why did you listen to me, why did you put up with my obstinacy!

She thought of the day when Apurba had caught her in his arms, on the lonely path by the edge of the pond and had looked deeply into her eyes without saying anything. She remembered the setting, the pond, the path, the trees, the morning sunlight and that sorrowful look and now she understood it all! She then thought of that day of departure when a kiss had almost reached Apurba's lips but had remained incomplete. The unfinished kiss now kept seeking out that day like a thirsty bird an oasis, never to be quenched. She often thought, if only I had done this, if only I had said that, what if!

Apurba was saddened by the thought that Mrinmoyee did not attempt to know him while she was pained by what he must have thought of her. The fact that he knew her only as an incorrigible, naughty, stupid unthinking child and not as a complete woman who was capable of fulfilling his thirst for love with her sweetness made her cringe in shame and repentance. She would try to compensate this with loving kisses showered on his pillow. Many days passed like this.

Apurba had said he would not return unless she wrote. Mrinmoyee remembered this and wrote a letter to him one day after barring the doors to her room. She took out the golden edged paper that Apurba had given her to write on. She took great care and somehow made the wobbly lines straight. With inky fingers she wrote without formally addressing anyone in letters of various sizes:

Why do you not write to me? How are you? And come home.

She could not think of anything else to write. She had said all that was really important, but it was essential that she write some more. She too understood this and after pondering this for a long time wrote:

You write to me, and write how you are, and come home. Ma is fine, Bishu and Puti are fine and yesterday the black cow had a calf.

She then finished the letter by sealing the envelope and writing Sri Babu Apurbakrishna Ray, and dotting the top of each letter with her love. In spite of all the love, the lines were not straight, the letters were not well formed and the spellings left much to be desired.

Mrinmoyee was not aware that one had to write anything apart from the name on the envelope. Ashamed that her mother-in-law would see the letter, she secretly gave it to a maid to post.

Needless to say, this letter did not have the desired effect and Apurba did not come home.

His mother noticed the holidays had started but Apurba did not come home. She thought he was still upset with her.

Mrinmoyee too decided that Apurba remained annoyed with her and felt mortified when she remembered her letters to him. Those letters were so insignificant; they had not said anything at all, she had not been able to say what she had felt and Apurba must have thought her so childish and would surely despise her even more now. All these thoughts made her burn with shame. She asked the maid again and again, 'Did you drop that letter in the post box?' 'Of course, with my own hands, he must have received it by now,' answered the maid.

Eventually Apurba's mother said to her one day, 'Child, he has not come home for such a long time. I was thinking I might go and visit him in Kolkata. Will you come with me?' Mrinmoyee nodded her head in agreement and then went to her room, locked the door, fell upon the bed and hugged her pillow in silent laughter. When she stopped, she grew serious and sadly thought about all the things that might have gone wrong; eventually she started crying.

These two remorseful women went to Kolkata to seek Apurba's forgiveness, without letting him know about it. They stayed with his sister.

That day, Apurba had given up any hope of receiving a letter from Mrinmoyee and had gone back on his own word by writing to her. Nothing seemed appropriate. He was looking for a form of address that was at once loving and indicative of his own sadness. He was at the stage where he had started to despair of his language, as it seemed to lack such a word. A letter arrived from his brother-in-law saying that his mother was staying with them and that he was to go to their house and have dinner with them that night. Everyone was well—inspite of this reassurance Apurba grew apprehensive and unhappy. He went to his sister's house without delay.

As soon as he saw his mother, he asked, 'Ma, is everything alright?' His mother answered, 'Everything is fine. You never came during the holidays, so I decided to come and take you home.'

Apurba said, 'Why did you have to come all the way, my examinations in Law…' and so on.

While they ate, his sister asked, 'Why did you not bring my sister-in-law with you?'

He answered with a serious face, 'My Law examinations...' and stated other such reasons.

Her husband laughed and said, 'these are all false excuses. He is scared of what Mrinmoyee might think on meeting us!'

She said, 'Well that is true! A child might get startled on seeing you.'

They all laughed and joked but Apurba felt very depressed. Nothing could make him feel happy. He thought that Mrinmoyee could easily have accompanied his mother, seeing that she had come to Kolkata after all. Possibly his mother had asked her but she would certainly have refused. He could not ask his mother anything more out of shyness—his whole life and the world seemed to have become a minefield of errors.

After they had eaten, a strong wind rose and it started raining heavily.

'Stay here with us today,' requested his sister.

He answered, 'No, I should go home, I have lots to do.'

His brother-in-law observed jocularly, 'What work do you hope to do at night? It is not as if you have to answer to anyone if you do happen to spend a night here. What is your problem?'

After many more requests and entreaties Apurba did agree to stay the night, although it was completely against his will.

His sister remarked, 'You are looking tired, let us not keep you up any longer and show you to your room.'

Apurba was also keen to retire; he was not feeling very sociable and all he wanted was to be resting in bed.

When they came to the door to the bedroom, they found it all dark. His sister said, 'It seems the wind has blown the lamp out. Will you need a light at all?'

Apurba said, 'No, I do not keep a night light on.'

When she left, Apurba carefully made his way to the bed in the darkness.

As he was about to lie down, a soft arm suddenly encircled him with a tinkle of bracelets in a tight embrace and a pair of petal soft lips fell upon him, bestowing an endless bounty of passionate kisses that took him by complete surprise. At first Apurba was startled but he soon realised that something that had once been left unfinished in laughter was finally being fulfilled in tears of joy.

(Samapti – Golpo Guchcho)

The Accidental Meeting

I saw her suddenly on the train
I had never felt it possible again.

I had seen her many times before
In a red sari
As bright as a pomegranate blossom
Today she was in black silk
The sari wrapped around her head
Around the glowing fair face so like a champaka flower
I felt the black created a distance between the two of us;
The same distance that colours the sal forest
That smudges the horizon at the end of the mustard fields.

My heart stood still for a moment
I saw the familiar in the guise of the unknown.

She put the newspaper aside at once
To greet me
Social mores satisfied,
We started to talk
How are you, how is your family etc?
She kept looking out of the window
As if she was looking beyond the recent past
She spoke little—a word or two,
Sometimes none at all.
Her restless hands spoke to me
Why all these words they said,
It would have been far better to have remained quiet.

I was sitting on another seat
With her companions
At one point she beckoned me to come close,
I felt this was very bold
I went and sat next to her.

Behind the sound of the train
Came her voice very low,
'Do not mind,
There is hardly any time to waste
I have to get off at the next station;
You will go further,
We will never meet again
That is why the answer that has stayed unsaid
I wish to hear
Will you tell me the truth?'
I said, 'I will'.

She kept looking at the sky as she said
'The days that we had
Are they completely finished?
Is there nothing left in them?'

I was silent for a little while.
Then I said,
'All the stars of the night lie in wait,
Lending their aura to the bright light of day.'

I felt strange, wondering, was I telling myself the truth?
She said, 'Alright, now go back over there'.
They all got off at the next stop.I went on, all alone.

(Hotat Dekha – 24th June 1936)

Green Mangoes

Three green mangoes lay under the tree
In the soft morning sun of Chaitra.
When I saw them, no longer
Did my hand reach for them anxious, eager.
I mused over my cup of tea,
How the wind has changed for me
The far bank grows blurred with time.
There were days when a fateful find of a green mango or two
Were like a golden key in my hands,
Opening the door to a secret chamber of happiness,
Today that lock broken, that key is not needed at all.

Let me begin where I should.

When in my youth a new bride arrived
The first time from another family

My mind was an anchored boat
Shaken from its moorings forever by flood.

The monotonous rationing of life
Overwhelmed by the generosity of fortune.
The old torn commonplace days and nights
Fell away from the whole house.
The constant strains of joyous shehnai
Changed the dialect of daily tedium
Each room filled with a cacophony of light
From chandeliers and crystal shades.
In the midst of the very familiar
Blossomed the intensely surprising.

Someone arrived in a burst of colour
Stepping on red painted soles
Telling the world that she was not to be
Measured by our usual rules.
That day she stood alone, beyond compare.
In a boy's eyes awoke a realisation
That there are things one can see yet not know.

The flutes stopped their music, the message did not.
Our bride stayed on too
Surrounded by an aura of wonder.

Her friendship, her fights, her play was with the sister-in-law.
I wanted to draw close to her, a little, with much shyness
Her sari patterns seemed to swirl around in my mind

But it did take but one frown to let me know,
I was a child, not a girl, a different species.

She was my age, one or two months
Older possibly, or perhaps younger.
I did have to accept that we
Were made by a different alchemy.
My mind sought to perhaps give something
Build a bridge into her heart.

Once this fool found a way
Strands of bright beads
Thinking to amaze with that borrowed brilliance.
She laughed and said, 'What Do I do with these!'
These tragedies do not find
Any recognition in history,
But a boy spent the rest of that day
Crushed under the weight of his shame.
Who will judge today
Those beads did have much value.

Yet in the midst of that was clear, cheap gifts were not
Completely unwelcome to this enthroned being
In that she was anchored to the earth.

She loved eating green mangoes
Dusted with red hot chilies and shulgo leaf.
There was still one small door left open
Even for a boy who was also a child
Climbing trees was strictly forbidden.

As soon as the wind rose, I would run
To the garden where if fate allowed me one fallen fruit
I would look upon it in momentary hesitation, how green,
How smooth, how beautiful that gift of nature.
The one who would devour it with greed
Would not see its wonderful form.

Once I had gathered the fruits while hail showered,
She said, 'Has anyone asked you to do this?'
I said, 'No one.'
I threw the basket down on the ground
And came away.
Another day, I was stung by a bee,
She said, 'There is no need to bring fruit like this.'
I remained quiet.

I grew older.
One day I received a golden ring from her
There was a message worth remembering engraved within.
When I bathed in the river
It slipped off and I never found it.

Even today, green mangoes fall with soft thuds
Under the tree, year after year.
The path to reaching her is gone forever.

(Kancha Aam – Santiniketan 8th April 1939)

The Uninvited

Early one morning, two boys stood by the side of the road, discussing a wager over an incredible feat of bravery. They were arguing about who was brave enough to gather flowers from the vine that draped along the walls of the nearby temple.

One said, 'I can', to which his friend claimed skeptically, 'Never.'

Even though this task sounds easy the reality was somewhat different; this needs to be explained in some more detail.

The widow of the late Madhab Chandra Tarkabachaspati, Joykali Devi was the caretaker of this Radhanath Jiu temple. Even though the late teacher had achieved the title of Tarkabachaspati in his career, he had never been able to prove his prowess at the art of debate against his wife. Some wags commented that the title had been well deserved as both Tarka (debate) and Bachya (word) had been given to his wife in ample measure and the good teacher had also borne the brunt of that while he was alive.

To be honest it must be said that though Joykali never said much, on many occasions she had been known to quell the most garrulous torrent of speech with one or two words, or even merely her stern silence.

She was a tall, strong, intelligent woman with a patrician nose. Their land holdings had been all but lost while her husband was alive. She had sorted out all the problems by collecting all overdue taxes, getting boundaries demarcated correctly and evicting all squatters from their land. No one could cheat her of a single paisa that was rightfully hers.

The many masculine traits in her character meant that she did not have suitable companions. Much of her own gender feared her. She could not bear gossip, idle banter, and opportunistic tears. Men were also afraid of her, because with one silent and sharp look she could express her intense disapproval of the long lazy hours they spent sitting in the village square in a way that pierced them, even through their thick-skinned indolence.

This elderly widow had an extraordinary ability to intensely dislike and to convey that dislike very severely indeed. If she judged someone to have done wrong, she would deliver her burning reproach both verbally and wordlessly, in behaviour as well as through actions.

She was however tireless in providing her help whenever the village folk needed it, in both sorrow and in celebration. When the need arose, no matter what the place, she was able to very easily take up a position of leadership and wherever she went, neither she nor anyone else present ever doubted that she was the one who was best suited to overseeing the event.

She was very proficient at tending to the sick, but they feared her as much as they feared death itself. If there was any lapse in following the doctor's orders or prescribed diets by the convalescent, her anger was far more likely to make her patient burn in remorse than the fever itself.

This tall, austere widow hung like a gavel of righteous justice above the villagers and no one had the courage to either ignore her or love her. She was involved in every affair of the hamlet but there was no one who was quite as lonely as her.

Though she was childless, she had two orphaned nephews who lived under her care. No one could say that there was any lessening of discipline in their lives due to the absence of a male guardian or that the blind adoration of their doting aunt had a detrimental effect on them in any manner.

The elder boy was about eighteen. Marriage proposals came for him on occasions and it needs to be said that he was not completely disinterested in establishing bonds of matrimony. But his aunt had paid no heed to these happy musings. Unlike other women, the gradual blossoming of love in the lives of a young couple did not seem like a very pleasant and enjoyable prospect to her way of thinking. In fact, she was disgusted by the possibility that her nephew might marry and like the other husbands of the village, spend his time at home growing in girth, thanks to his wife's affections.

She would say stonily, 'Let Pulin earn a living first! Then he can bring a wife home.'

The aunt's heartless declarations would crush the aspirations of the hopeful females in the village.

The temple was her most prized possession. There could be no lapses in the routine of offering prayers and preparing the food for the deity. The two Brahmin priests feared this one woman a great deal more than all the gods.

There had been one instance when the gods had not received their full dues. This was because one of the priests had another object he secretly worshipped, in the form of his paramour Nistarini. The daily offerings of clarified butter, milk, cream and flour were being distributed between the gods in heaven and the gates of hell. But these days, thanks to Joykali's control, the offerings were reaching their rightful place, and the demigoddess had to look elsewhere for sustenance.

The widow's care ensured that the temple courtyard was sparkling clean—not even a blade of grass could be seen growing out of place. On one side, a flowering vine climbed up the wall of the temple and as soon as it shed a dry leaf, Joykali was there to pick it up and throw it outside. The widow could not bear it if there was even the slightest disturbance to the neatness and sanctity of the temple. Earlier, the neighbourhood children used to enter the courtyard while playing hide-and-seek, and sometimes, even goat kids wandered in and nibbled at the bark at the base of the vine.

They never had that chance any more. The children were not allowed into the courtyard unless it was a festival and the hungry goat kid would scamper back to its mother, bleating plaintively, after being chastised with a stick before it had even entered the place.

Morally reprehensible people were denied entrance to the sacred courtyard even if they were close relatives. Once, a brother-in-law of hers had come to visit, and the said relative was rather fond of chicken dishes prepared by the hands of heathens. Even before he'd stepped foot in the temple, Joykali's promptly and sharply expressed protest had almost led to an estrangement with her own sister.

She was so excessively and needlessly careful about the temple that other people thought it was largely a sign of insanity.

Joykali might have been immoveable and rigidly independent elsewhere but she had surrendered herself completely to the temple. She was mother, wife and servant to the deity—before it she was watchful, soft, beautiful and completely servile. This stone temple and the stone idol within were the only place where her innermost hidden feminine nature was able to find fulfillment. This was indeed her husband, her son, her all.

From this the reader will understand that the boy who was pledging to pick flowers from the courtyard was brave indeed. He was her younger nephew Nalin. He knew his aunt well enough, but his incorrigible nature had not been conquered by her disciplinary measures. He yearned to be where there was danger and his heart grew keen whenever there were rules to be broken. It was rumoured that his aunt had been the same in her childhood.

When it happened, Joykali had been gazing upon the idol with a mixture of maternal feeling and reverence, as she sat before it, counting the beads on her rosary.

The boy came with silent steps from behind and stood at the base of the vine.

He saw that the flowers on the lowest branches had been taken for the ceremonies so he started to climb. Carefully and very slowly, he scaled the wall, but the inevitable happened.

There he was, stretching his body and arm out to pluck the few opening buds on the upper branches, when the flimsy support gave way under that great effort and collapsed, taking the vine and the boy with it.

Joykali came quickly, and seeing what her nephew had done, wrenched him upright by his arm. He had been hurt, but that could not be called a punishment as it was at the hands of an unknowing adversary.

So, Joykali, knowingly, began raining blows upon the boy's injured body.

Her nephew bore these silently without shedding a single tear. Once the beating was over, she dragged him into a room and locked him inside. It was decided that he would not be given his afternoon meal.

When the maid, Mokkhoda, heard that he was being denied his food, she tearfully begged for forgiveness on his behalf. This did nothing to soothe Joykali's heart and no one in the household was foolhardy enough to secretly give the hungry boy food without his aunt's knowledge.

The widow sent for people to come and repair the support and sat down again in the courtyard.

Mokkhoda came to her after a while and said fearfully, 'Grandmother, the young boy is crying in hunger, shall I take some milk to him?'

With an unperturbed face, 'No', was all Joykali said.

Mokkhoda went back. From the nearby room, Nalin's plaintive cries gradually turned into roars of anger, and as time dragged on, when he'd subsided into cries of exhaustion, he could still be heard by his aunt.

When Nalin's pained cries had almost ceased, the frightened calls of another animal could be made out over the faraway shouts of a mob of men folk running.

The din was growing louder as it drew nearer, until a tremendous cacophony was heard on the path outside the temple.

Suddenly, footsteps were heard within the courtyard. Joykali turned to see that the fallen vine was being shaken by something.

She angrily called out her nephew's name, 'Nalin?'

No one replied. She thought that the stubborn Nalin had somehow escaped from his imprisonment and was trying to annoy her further.

Biting her lip in anger, she came down to the courtyard.

When she was close to the vine, she called out again, 'Nalin?'

There was no answer. She lifted a branch to find an extremely dirty pig hiding in the dense foliage, in fear of its life.

How could such a horrifying event have happened in this little piece of Vrindavan enclosed by brick walls, where the vine grew, and the perfume of its flowers reminded all of the sweet breath of the gopis, the milkmaids and brought dreams of the bliss that was to be found only by the banks of the Kalindi, in this most treasured of her possessions?

The Brahmin priest came running, ready to chase away the animal with a stick.

Joykali immediately stepped forward and ordered him to stop. She locked the gate from the inside, and soon enough, the drunken band of Doms arrived at the other side of the gate and started asking for their prey in loud voices.

Joykali stated from behind the barred doors, 'Go away wretches! Do not defile my temple!'

The band of Doms turned back.

Even though they had seen the pig enter the temple with their own eyes, they could hardly believe that Joykali would allow such an unclean animal to take shelter in her sacred temple.

Even though the god of all living things great and small on Earth was greatly happy at this trivial incident, the extremely insignificant force that was the society of this little village was extremely angered by this.

(Awnodhikar Probesh – Golpo Guchcho)

The Dowry

When a daughter arrived after five brothers, her parents named her Nirupama, (The Incomparable). Such a fanciful name had never been heard of in this family before. The general trend so far had been to name children after the gods—Ganesh, Kartick, Parvati etc.

We enter this story as Nirupama's marriage is being planned. Her father Ramsundor Mitra had been looking far and wide but none of the grooms were to his liking. Finally he found a prospective husband, the only child of a great official, a Raibahadur. Even though the family had lost most of their former wealth, they were still aristocratic in their tastes.

They demanded ten thousand rupees and a large number of gifts as a dowry. Ramsundor agreed to these conditions without giving it much thought. After all, it would be insane to lose such a son-in-law.

He found it very difficult to borrow the money. Even after pawning and selling off many of the family possessions, he was still short of six to seven thousand rupees. In the mean time, the day of the marriage drew closer.

Finally the day of the marriage dawned. A lender who had agreed to give Ramsundor the money he needed—but at a very high rate of interest—failed to materialise. There was a tremendous uproar where everyone was assembled. Ramsundor prostrated himself at the great official's feet saying, 'Let the festivities be completed, I will surely give you the money in full.'

The official declared, 'The groom will not sit down for the ceremony unless we are given the full amount.'

This unfortunate turn of events caused a wailing to break out in the inner rooms of the house. The person who was the chief reason behind this mishap was sitting quietly wrapped in a red silk saree and jewellery, her forehead smeared with ritual marks in sandalwood paste. I cannot say that she was feeling a great sense of respect or love towards her would be parents-in-law.

In the mean time, something good had happened. The groom suddenly decided to oppose his father's ruling and said, 'I do not understand this talk of buying, selling and pricing. I came here to get married and that is what I intend to do.'

His father said to anyone who would listen, 'Have you seen such a thing, boys these days!' Some elderly people there said, 'What else do you expect, with a lack of education in the scriptures and ethics.'

The great official sat in one place, dumbfounded at the evil effects of modern education on his own son. The marriage took place with an air of gloom and unhappiness surrounding it.

Before Nirupama went to her new home, her father could not hold his tears back anymore as he embraced her. She asked, 'Will they not let me come and visit, Father?' Ramsundor said, 'Why not, Ma! I will go and fetch you myself.'

Ramsundor went to see his daughter quite often but he had no standing in that house. Even the servants treated him with scorn. He was able to see her for a few minutes in a separate outer room sometimes, and not even that at others.

This insult at the hands of his kinsmen was beyond bearing. Ramsundor decided he was going to pay the remainder of the dowry somehow.

But the debts he had already incurred were very hard to maintain. He was continually short of money and was having to use a number of low ruses to evade his creditors.

His daughter too was reminded of the circumstances of the wedding at every opportunity by her in-laws. Weeping behind closed doors at the abuse of her father and brothers became a daily occurrence.

Her mother-in-law's anger was especially insatiable. If anyone remarked, 'Such beauty! Your daughter-in-law's face is like balm to my eyes,' she would angrily say, 'What of her beauty! She looks like a daughter of a poor family, no better, no less!'

No one paid much attention to Niru's most basic needs for food and clothing. When a kindly neighbour remarked on the neglect, her mother-in- law said, 'We are doing enough for her.' As if she would have received complete care if only her father had paid the full price! Everyone behaved as though she had no rights there; that she had tricked her way into their home.

News of the neglect and misbehaviour that his daughter was being subjected to possibly reached Ramsundor. He eventually decided to sell the family home.

He did not let his sons know that he was about to make them homeless. He had decided that he would rent the house back after selling it; this would be a way of concealing the truth until the time of his death.

But his sons did come to know. They came to him tearfully. Especially his three married sons who had children of their own. They protested their father's plans most vehemently and the sale was postponed.

Niru could understand everything from the look on her father's face. The pressures of poverty and worry were evident in the old man's white hair, his drawn features and his constantly apologetic manner. When a father has wronged his daughter, it is impossible to hide the guilt. When he was allowed to see her for a few moments with the kind permission of her new family, his smile was enough proof of the heart-wrenching grief he inwardly felt.

She became desperate to go home and comfort his pain for a few days. She could hardly stay away after witnessing his dejected face. She said to him one day, 'Please take me home once.' Ramsundor replied, 'I will.'

But he had no influence—even the usual rights that a father can claim of having a daughter's company seemed to have been handed over in exchange for the unpaid dowry. Even for seeing her, he had to ask with a great deal of trepidation and when refused, was unable to ask a second time.

But how can a father not bring a daughter home when she herself wants to go? It is best that I do not disclose what nature of abuse, deprivation and insults Ramsundor had to bear before he managed to get together the required three thousand rupees before he could even state his plea in front of the great official.

He had the notes tied up in a handkerchief that he was carefully carrying, as he went and sat down before his daughter's father-in-law. He began by talking about various local events with a smile. He described in great detail a robbery that had taken place at Harekrishna's house. He then proceeded to compare the brothers Nabinmadhab and Radhamadhab, praising Radhamadhab for his intelligence and nature and decrying Nabinmadhab for the lack of the same. He talked at great length about a strange new disease that was afflicting people in town. Finally he put the hookah down and said, 'You know that money for the dowry. I do seem to recall there is some of it still owing to you. I think of bringing it over each time I visit you, but I keep forgetting. Such is old age.' After saying this, he held out the three notes like three of his own ribs with an air of affected disdain. The great official roared with laughter at the sight of just three thousand rupees.

He said, 'That is quite alright, I can do without that.' He alluded to a vernacular proverb about not wanting to soil his hands for such a paltry reason.

There was no question of raising a demand to bring Niru home after this—but Ramsundor felt, 'The rules that govern behaviour in these circumstances do not apply to me.' After sitting in a state of shocked silence for a while he stated his actual reason for being there. The Raibahadur did not say anything beyond, 'That will not be possible at this moment.' He then left the room.

Ramsundor picked up the notes with a trembling hand and went home without seeing Niru. He pledged to himself that he would not go back as long as he had not managed to get together the entire sum of money and ask for his daughter without hesitation.

Many days passed. Nirupama kept sending people to enquire after her father but he would not come and see her. Eventually, she grew hurt and stopped sending people—this caused Ramsundor much pain, but he still would not go to visit her.

The month of Ashwin came. Ramsundor promised himself, 'This time, if I am not successful at bringing her home, I will surely....' He made an unbreakable promise to himself.

On the fifth or sixth day of the fortnight of the festival, he again prepared to go to Niru's home with the money tied in a handkerchief.

His five-year-old grandson came to him and said, 'Are you going to buy me a cart?' He had a desire to ride in a cart for a long time but this wish had not been fulfilled. A six-year-old grand daughter came and tearfully told him that she did not have anything fit to wear if she was invited.

Ramsundor knew all this and he had been thinking a lot about this, as he smoked his hookah. He had fretted and sighed a lot over the lack of new jewellery and clothes for his daughter-in-law, when he would go to the great official's house. This had done nothing but deepen the worry lines on his forehead.

With the sounds of his own poverty-stricken household ringing in his ears, the old man went to his daughter's home. Today he was not hesitant anymore; he looked the gatekeeper and the servants in the eye without furtive shy glances as though he was entering his own house. He heard that he would have to wait a while as the Raibahadur was not at home. He went to see Niru as he was unable to hold back his emotions. His eyes overflowed with tears of joy. Father and daughter both wept without speaking. Some time passed before he could say, 'This time I am taking you with me, and there should be no problem with that.'

Suddenly Ramsundor's eldest son Haramohan entered the room with his two young children. He asked, 'Father, have you then forsaken us completely?'

Ramsundor became enraged and said, 'Will I have to go to hell for your sake? Will you not let me keep my promise?' He had sold the house secretly, making arrangements so that his sons remained in the dark, but he was extremely angry to discover that they had still found out.

His grandson grabbed his knees and looked up at him, saying, 'Grandfather, you did not buy the cart for me?'

Having not had a reply from Ramsundor who was sitting with a bowed head, the child then went to Niru and said, 'Aunt, will you buy me a cart?'

Nirupama understood what was happening and said, 'Father, if you give any more money to my father-in-law, I promise you, you will never see me again!'

Ramsundor said, 'No, you must never say that. If I do not give this money, it is an insult to both your father and to you.'

Niru said, 'It is more of an insult if you do pay. Do I have no honour? Am I just a money bag, to be loved as long as I am full? No, do not insult me with this money, and besides, my husband has not asked for this money.'

Ramsundor said, 'Then they will not let you go, dear.'

Nirupama said, 'What can you do if they do not allow me to go. Do not ask them any more.'

Ramsundor shakily picked up the notes and left for home surreptitiously like a thief.

The fact that Ramsundor had brought the money and that he had returned without handing it over at his daughter's behest was not to remain a secret for long. Some eavesdropping servant went and gave Niru's mother-in-law the news. She became angrier than ever.

The house became a bed of thorns for Niru. Her husband had been given a posting as a Deputy Magistrate and had left for his place of work within a few days of the marriage. Her contact with her own family was completely banned on the grounds of moral corruption.

At this time Niru became very ill. Her mother-in-law cannot be held entirely responsible for this. Niru took very little care of herself. She would leave the shutters open all night on the bitterly cold nights of the month of Kartick in winter when she denied herself warm clothing. There was no routine to her meals. When the servants occasionally forgot to bring her food to her, she never once said a word to remind them. Her firm belief was that she was completely dependent on the kindness of the elders and the servants of another family, not the one that had accepted her. Her mother-in-law could not bear this either. When she perceived disdain for the food in Niru's manner, she said, 'She is from a Nawab's family! Why should this ordinary food be to her liking?' At other times she would say, 'Look at her! She looks more like a withered piece of firewood as each day passes.'

When the illness took a turn for the worse, her mother-in-law said 'These are all pretences'

Eventually one day Niru said to her politely, 'I would like to see my father and brothers just once, Mother.'

Her mother-in-law replied, 'Conniving to go home again!'

I know no one will believe this—the day that Niru breathed her last was also the day the doctor was summoned to the house, to see her for the first and last time.

The eldest daughter-in-law had died; therefore the funeral took place with great pomp. Just as the Ray Chowdhury family of the region were renowned for the splendid manner of their deity immersions, the official's family became famous—no one had seen such a pyre of sandalwood in the area ever before. Such a grand funeral was only possible in a family of such standing and I have heard he incurred a small debt as a result of all of this.

Everyone consoled Ramsundor with vivid descriptions of how grand his daughter's manner of death had been.

The deputy magistrate wrote home, 'I have arranged everything here, kindly send my wife without further delay.' The great official's wife wrote back, 'Son, we have organised another bride for you, you must come here with a few days leave.'

This time there was a dowry of twenty thousand rupees and it was promptly collected.

(Dena Paona – Golpo Guchcho)

The Living and the Dead

The landlord of Ranihat, Zamindar Sharadashankarbabu had a sister-in-law who had no one left in her father's family as they had all passed away one by one. She had also lost her husband as well as her son, so she did not really have anyone on her husband's side of the family either. Her nephew, Sharadashankar's younger son, was the apple of her eye. Saradashankar had been her husband's elder brother. The boy's mother was ill for a long time after his birth and this widowed aunt Kadambini had helped raise him. When a person raises another's child, the pull is greater because it is not a relationship recognised by society but one of love—these bonds cannot be proved with legal documentation and neither do they need to; they just bind with twice the intensity as one is never certain of how long the object of love will remain so.

After giving up all the love suppressed within her widowed heart to this boy, Kadambini suddenly died one rainy night. The reason behind this was uncertain and everything else in the world went on as it always had, only the wheels of time spinning inside that insignificant gentle loving heart stopped forever.

Fearful that the police would raise questions over this, the zamindar organised four Brahmin employees to take the body away to be cremated quickly and without much ceremony.

The cremation grounds in Ranihat were far from the village houses. There was but one hut by the pond. Nearby, there stood a massive banyan tree in the middle of a vast empty field. A long time ago, a river had flowed through the place but that was dry today. A section of the ancient river bed had been excavated to create a pond next to the cremation grounds. Local people revered it as a symbol of the old river.

The four waited with the body in the hut for the pyre wood to arrive. It took so long that two of them, Nitai and Gurucharan, went to see what the reason behind the delay was. Bidhu and Bonomali stayed back to guard the corpse.

It was a dark rainy night in the month of Shravan. Dense clouds filled the skies and not a star could be seen as the two men waited quietly in that dark room. One had a taper and matches but try as he might, the wet matches refused to light—even the lantern they had with them went out after a while.

After waiting for a long time one said, 'Brother, you know what would have been good? A few draws of tobacco. I forgot to bring that in the rush.'

The other replied, 'I could quickly go and get some.'

Bidhu understood that Bonomali was planning to escape and said, 'Bloody hell! Am I to wait here alone?'

There was silence once again. Five minutes felt like an hour. The ones in the room began cursing, the more they thought about the ones who had gone off in search of wood—it became obvious that they were sitting in some dry spot, happily smoking tobacco.

There were no other sounds apart from the monotonous calls of crickets and frogs from the banks of the pond. Around this time, it seemed as if the litter moved a bit, as though the corpse had turned on its side.

Bidhu and Bonomali tremulously started to say the Lord's name. A ghostly sigh was heard in the room and they wasted no more time in jumping up and running away as fast as they could in the direction of the village.

A couple of miles away, they met the other two coming along with a lantern. They truly had gone in search of smokes, and knew nothing about the firewood, but lied that the wood was being chopped and would arrive shortly. Bidhu and Bonomali then described the entire incident to them. Nitai and Gurucharan laughed in disbelief and furiously rebuked the others for neglecting their responsibilities.

The four of them wasted no more time and went back to the hut at the cremation ground. There they found nothing but an empty litter.

They looked at each other. What if jackals had dragged the body away? But even the shroud was gone. As they looked for clues as to what might have happened, they saw fresh prints of a woman's delicate feet in some mud outside the door of the hut.

Sharadashankar was not an easy man to fool; he would not believe this ghostly tale. The four, therefore, decided to go and tell him that the cremation had taken place.

When the wood finally arrived at dawn, they were told the cremation had already been carried out with wood that was stored in the hut. No one doubted this statement as a dead body is hardly a thing of value worth stealing.

Everyone knows that sometimes even when there are no signs of life, it can be there and an apparently lifeless body can start walking again. Kadambini had not died—for some reason, her body had appeared lifeless.

When she regained consciousness, she saw it was dark all around her. She understood that she was not in her own familiar bed. She once called out, 'Sister!' but no one answered back from the darkness. She sat up in alarm, remembering her sickbed. The sudden pains in her chest and a feeling of suffocation, her sister-in-law sitting in a corner of the room, warming milk for the child on a fire, Kadambini unable to stand a minute longer and falling upon the bed from where she begged her sister-in-law hoarsely, 'Sister, please bring the boy to me, I feel very strange.' And then all grew dark—like an inkwell tipping on to a page full of writing—her memories and her consciousness, all the letters in the book of her existence blended into that pool of darkness. The widow could not even remember if the child had called her Aunt in his sweet loving tones or not, or whether she had managed to bring one last vestige of love from her familiar world on this eternal yet unknown journey towards death.

At first she felt the land of the dead was probably always empty and dark. There was nothing to see there, nor anything to hear, nothing to do, nothing at all except remain awake.

Then when a cold breeze came through the open door and she heard the frog calls of the season, all the memories of rain from her short life came flooding back and she felt the close touch of the world that she belonged to. A flash of lightning illuminated the pond, the banyan tree, the emptiness beyond and the distant tree-lined horizon. She remembered how she had come to bathe in this pond on religious occasions and how death had seemed horrifying when she saw the dead bodies at this cremation ground.

At first, she thought of returning home. Immediately she thought, 'I am no longer alive, why would they accept me? It would be unlucky for them. I am banished from the land of the living—for I am my own ghost.'

If that was not the case why was she brought here miles away from Sharadashankar's secure house to this remote cremation ground? If she had not been already cremated, where were the people meant to do that? She remembered the lighted rooms where she had spent the last minutes of her life and then immediately thought of the empty darkness that now surrounded her in this faraway place. She now knew, 'I am no longer a part of this world of people—I am terrifying, malevolent, I am my own ghost.'

As soon as she thought this, the bonds that held her within the rules of the world seemed to fall away as if she had unusual strength and endless freedom—she could go where she wished and do what she wanted. As this unfamiliar feeling enveloped her, she became delirious and walked out of the room like a rush of wind into the dark cremation ground without a trace of fear.

As she walked, her feet tired and her strength waned. She walked through field after field, rice growing in some, knee deep water in others. When the dawn light finally broke, a bird or two could be heard in the bamboo groves of the nearby villages.

Then she started to feel afraid. She did not know what new relationship she would now have with the living people of the world. While she was in the fields, in the cremation ground, or enveloped in the darkness of the rainy night, she was unafraid, as though in her own kingdom. The village in the light of day seemed like a terrifying place for her. Humans fear ghosts just as ghosts fear humans, living as we do on the two banks of the river of death.

Her clothes covered in mud, her face in the grip of various emotions and maddened by the experiences of the night was a sight which would have frightened people and attracted stones and clods from children. Thankfully, she was first seen by a passing gentleman.

He said to her, 'Mother, you look like a woman of a respectable family, where are you going alone in such a condition?'

Kadambini did not answer at first and kept staring at him. She could not think of what to say. It seemed unbelievable that she was in a world where she was still thought of as a respectable woman and that a passerby was talking to her.

The traveller said to her again, 'Come Mother, let me take you home, tell me where your home is.'

She began to think that she could not go back to her husband's family and she had no one of her own; then she remembered her childhood friend.

Even though she had not seen Jogmaya since childhood, they had written to each other occasionally. At one stage they both competed to show that they were each more faithful than the other. Kadambini wanted to prove that she felt greater affection, while Jogmaya thought she was a greater friend and Kadambini was unable to match her. If there was ever a chance of them meeting, they both felt certain that it would be impossible to be apart for even the shortest while.

Kadambini told the gentleman, 'I wish to go to Sripaticharan babu's house in Nishindapur.'

The traveller was bound for Kolkata; even though Nishindapur was far away, it lay on his route and he made arrangements to take Kadambini to Sripaticharan babu's house himself.

The two friends met. At first they could not recognise each other but then childhood features became more apparent and they both remembered the other.

Jogmaya said, 'How lucky am I! I never thought I would ever see you. But how did you come here? How did they let you leave on your own?'

Kadambini was quiet and finally said, 'Please do not ask me about my in-laws. Just let me stay like a servant in a corner of your house. I will work for you all.'

Jogmaya exclaimed, 'What! Why do you say that? Why would you be a servant? You are my friend, you are my…'

At this time Sripati entered the room. Kadambini stared at his face for a while and slowly left the room—she showed no signs of covering her head out of shame or respect.

Jogmaya began to try and convince Sripati in various ways, so that he would not misunderstand her friend. But she had to say little before Sripati agreed to all her demands so readily that she was left quite dissatisfied.

Kadambini came to her friend's home but she could not rekindle the old relationship—death had come to stand between them. If one is continually suspicious and conscious of one's own existence, it is hard to blend with others. Kadambini would look at Jogmaya and think of something—of the distant world she inhabited with her husband and her household. 'With all the love, affection and responsibilities she has, she is of this world, whereas I am just an empty shell. She lives in the present whereas I roam the endless spheres,' Kadambini thought.

Jogmaya thought it all very peculiar but she could not understand it. Women cannot stand mysteries—because one can be poetic, brave, even wise about things beyond the realm of certainty, but one cannot be domestic. This is why when women do not understand something, they either pretend that it does not exist and refuse all dealings with it or they give it a new form of their own liking and make it something that they can make use of. If they cannot do either of the two, they grow very annoyed with it.

The more inscrutable Kadambini became, the angrier Jogmaya grew, wondering, 'What kind of a hassle is this!'

Another problem was that Kadambini was afraid of herself. She could not escape from herself, try as she might. Those who fear ghosts are most afraid of what lies behind them—the unseen is the most fearsome. But her fears all lay within—she feared nothing on the outside.

This is why, some times in the lonely midday hours she would scream aloud in fright—and in the evenings she would tremble to see her own shadows in the flickering lamplight.

This fear infected the minds of the people in the house as well. Jogmaya and her staff started seeing ghosts every now and again.

One day it became so bad that Kadambini woke in the middle of the night and knocked on Jogmaya's door, weeping, 'Sister, please! I beg you! Do not leave me alone!'

Jogmaya was both frightened and angered in equal measure. She felt like throwing Kadambini out of her house at that very moment. Kindhearted Sripati calmed her down and gave Kadambini the room next door to stay in.

The next day, Sripati was summoned to the inner house at an odd hour. Jogmaya saw him and immediately rebuked him saying, 'What kind of a man are you! A woman has been living here in your house for over a month, she does not speak once of leaving and going back to her husband's home and yet you have not spoken out once against that. Tell me what is going on here. Are all men like this?'

In all honesty, men have a tendency to favour all women and this makes women find greater fault with them. Even though Sripati was prepared to swear by his wife that he did not feel a greater than normal sense of compassion for the forsaken but beautiful Kadambini, his behaviour indicated otherwise.

He used to think, 'The in-laws must have tormented this childless widow beyond bearing which is why she has sought my protection. When she has neither a father nor a mother, how can I forsake her?' This made him desist from trying to find out what had happened and he did not feel like asking her to explain this unpleasantness either.

His wife questioned his lack of responsible behaviour in various ways. He could well understand that it was extremely necessary for peace in his own home that he send word to Kadambini's family. Eventually he decided that rather than sending off a letter, he would go to Ranihat himself to find out what the next course of action should be.

When Sripati left, Jogmaya said to Kadambini, 'Dear friend, it is not right that you stay here any longer. What will people say?'

Kadambini stared at her unsmilingly and said, 'What do I care about people?'

Jogmaya was amazed to hear this. She said, slightly irritated, 'Even if you don't, we must. How can we keep someone else's daughter-in-law here?'

Kadambini said, 'Where is my in-law's house?'

Jogmaya thought, 'Oh my God! What is the wretch saying?'

Kadambini said slowly, 'Am I no one to you? Am I even of this world? You laugh, you cry, you love, all of you are happy with your own, I am just looking in. You are people, I am but a shadow. I do not understand why God has placed me in the middle of this family. You are afraid lest I bring ill will to your joy and I do not begin to understand what place I have in all this. But since he has not provided me with any other place of my own, I must roam this world of yours even though the bonds may feel loose at times.'

She said these words in such a manner that Jogmaya only understood some parts and could not answer her at all. She could not ask any other questions. She went away with a heavy heart.

It was almost ten at night when Sripati came back from Ranihat. The rain fell unceasingly, flooding the earth. The endless dripping did not make it seem like the rain or that night would ever end.

Jogmaya asked, 'What did you find out?'

Sripati said, 'Plenty. I will tell you later.' He then changed, had his dinner and had a smoke before going to bed. He appeared extremely worried.

Jogmaya, who had suppressed her curiosity for a long time, came to bed and asked immediately, 'Tell me what you heard.'

Sripati said, 'You must have made a mistake.'

Jogmaya felt rather annoyed when she heard this. Women never make mistakes and even if they do, a sensible man should not dwell on them and rather admit that they are in the wrong. Jogmaya asked with some rancour, 'How is that?'

Sripati said, 'That woman you are sheltering is not your friend Kadambini.'

Anyone would be annoyed at this—especially if one's own husband says it. Jogmaya said, 'I do not know my friend, you know her better! What a thing to say!'

Sripati tried to convince her that they were not arguing about whether it was the right thing to say, but about proof. There was no doubt that her friend Kadambini had died.

Jogmaya said, 'Listen! You have obviously made a mistake. You must have gone to the wrong place, misheard things and so on. Who asked you to go anyway, a letter would have been enough! All would have been clear.'

Sripati was extremely annoyed by his wife's lack of faith in him and tried to place all the proof in front of her, but to no avail. This discussion continued till after midnight.

Even though they were both unanimous in the idea that Kadambini would have to be thrown out of their home that very instant—Sripati because he thought she was an imposter, and Jogmaya because she thought Kadambini was a fallen woman—neither was prepared to admit defeat in the present argument.

Both continued to raise their voices, forgetting that Kadambini lay in the very next room.

One said, 'This is a fine situation! I heard it said with my own ears!'

The other said, 'Why should I accept that when I can see her here with my own eyes.'

Finally Jogmaya asked, 'Can you tell me when Kadambini died?'

She thought she would establish a discrepancy between her arrival and the dates on one of Kadambini's letters and prove Sripati wrong.

When Sripati told her the date, the two of them found that it was the very day before the day that Kadambini had come to their house. As soon as she heard this, she shivered in fright and Sripati felt rather uneasy as well.

Suddenly their door opened, a gust of wind rushed in and the lamp went out abruptly. The outer darkness came in and filled the room completely in a matter of seconds. Kadambini came and stood right inside the room. It was very late at night, outside the rain continued unabated.

Kadambini said, 'Sister, I am your Kadambini, but I am no longer of this world. I am dead.'

Jogmaya cried out in fear while Sripati was dumbstruck.

'But how have I wronged you apart from dying. If I have no place in this world or the next—where then will I go!' She cried out bitterly as if to awaken her sleeping fate on the dark rainy night, asking, 'Tell me, where can I go then?'

She then left the senseless couple in the darkened room and went to find her place in the world.

It is difficult to say how Kadambini managed to return to Ranihat. But she did not reveal herself to anyone at first. Although hungry, she hid in a ruined temple near the house all day.

When the early dusk of the season had congealed into solid darkness and all the villagers had gone indoors in haste in order to avoid the coming storm, Kadambini emerged from hiding and walked home. Her heart beat faster when she reached the door of her in-laws house but when she covered her face, the gatemen mistook her for a maid and she was free to enter. The rain and the winds grew in force at this time.

Saradashankar's wife was playing cards with her widowed sister-in-law at the time. The maid was in the kitchen and the sick child, who was rather weakened by fever, was sleeping in a bedroom by himself. Kadambini managed to reach that room undetected by anyone. I do not know how she managed the journey back home and even she would have been unable to tell us, but she did know that she wanted to see the child just once. What would happen after that, where she would go… these were things she had not thought about.

She saw the sickly child lying asleep, hands balled into fists. This sight filled her agitated mind with a thirst that would not be quenched unless she held him to her breast just once, despite all her problems. She also remembered, 'I have not been here, who knows who is looking after him? His mother loves the company of others, she loves gossip and games, and she was free to do all that without care while I was here. Who looks after him today, I wonder!'

Suddenly the child turned on his side and sleepily said, 'Aunt, give me a drink.' Her heart filled with love as she thought that her darling boy had not forgotten his aunt yet. She quickly poured a drink from the earthen jar and picked him up to give him the water.

As long as sleep had dulled his senses, the boy did not feel anything amiss while he drank the water she gave him. Eventually, when she kissed him and laid him back on the bed, he woke up and clung to her asking, 'Aunty, did you die?'

The aunt said, 'Yes, my child.'

'Have you come back to me again? You are not going to die anymore?'

Before she could answer him, a problem occurred—the maid was about to come in with a bowl of sago pudding and she took one look at the scene and screamed before falling down in a faint.

The scream brought the lady of the house running and she came into the room and froze. She could neither leave nor speak a single word.

All this frightened the child—who cried out, 'Aunty, please go away.'

After a long time, Kadambini realised today that she had not really died—the familiar house, with all its things, the child, her love, all these were as immediate as they had always been; there had been nothing to distance her from them. When Kadambini had gone to Jogmaya's house, she had found her childhood friend and she had thought herself dead. But now in the child's bedroom, she felt that she had not died at all.

She piteously said, 'Sister, why do you all fear me? See, I am just as I was before.'

The lady of the house could stand this no longer, she fainted too.

Saradashankar came to the bedroom after being informed by his sister—and said to Kadambini respectfully, 'Sister-in-law is this right, that you should cast your eyes on Satish who is our only descendant? Are we not your family? Since you passed away, he pines for you, he refuses to get better, and he asks for you day and night. Now that you are no longer a part of this life, you must give up these bonds—we will perform the appropriate rites for your spirit.'

Kadambini could no longer bear it and screamed, 'I have not died, truly, I have not. How do I convince you all? I have not died! Here, see, I am alive!'

She picked up a brass bowl from the floor and began hitting herself with it; her forehead began to bleed.

She then said, 'Can you not see, I am alive.'

Saradashankar stood motionless like a statue—the frightened child kept calling him and the two women lay on the ground senseless.

Kadambini then shrieked, 'I tell you, I did not die, I did not die!' and ran from the room, down the stairs and jumped into the pond behind the house. Saradashankar heard a splash from where he stood upstairs.

It rained that whole night, it was still raining the next morning—it was still raining at mid day. It took Kadambini's death to prove to the world that she had not died earlier.

(Jeebito o Mrito – Golpo Guchcho)

The Skeleton

A complete human skeletont used to hang on the wall of the room, next to the bedroom which I shared with two others while we were all children. Each night the bones clacked against each other in the wind and each day we looked at them and learned their names. We were studying the *Meghnadvadh* from a Sanskrit teacher and the science of bones from a student of the Campbell College. Our guardian wanted to turn us into experts in every field overnight. It is futile to speak of how far he was successful in this with those who know us and it is best to hide this from those who don't.

Much time has passed since then. The skeleton has disappeared from that room and the names of its bones have certainly disappeared from our memories, leaving no traces behind.

Recently I had to sleep in that room for a night as there was a shortage of beds in the house. I could not fall asleep easily as the arrangement was unfamiliar. As I tossed and turned, I listened to the church bells ringing out almost all the hours of the night. Suddenly, the oil lamp at the corner of the room seemed to gasp a few times before dying out completely. We already had a few unfortunate events in our family. Thus, the guttering of the lamp brought the thought of death quite naturally to my mind and I thought of how both this and the fading of the faint flames of human life were one and the same in nature.

I then began thinking of that skeleton. As I thought of how its life might have been, I sensed that a presence was wandering about the room, groping the walls of the room outside my mosquito net. I could hear its heavy breathing. It seemed to be looking for something and it moved faster and faster as it failed to find what it was seeking. I knew for certain that this was the effect of sleeplessness on my heated brain, but it still felt frightening. In an attempt to get over this irrational fear I said, 'Who is that?' The footsteps came to a halt outside the mosquito netting, and I heard an answering voice reply, 'It is I. I have come to look for that skeleton of mine.'

I knew it would not do to show my fear of something that I had invented myself—and so I held the bolster close and asked in a tone of great familiarity, 'What a thing to do at this hour! But why do you need it after so many years?'

There was an answer from very close to the bed. 'What are you saying! The bones that encased this heart are still there.

The dreams of twenty six summers that once blossomed around it—should I not want to see it once again?'

I answered promptly, 'Yes, the wish is justifiable. Well, go and look for it then—and let me sleep.'

It said, 'Are you by yourself? Then let me sit awhile. Let me talk to you for a short while. Thirty five years ago, I too used to sit by people and talk with people. But I have wandered on the empty winds of the burning grounds in the years since. Let me sit with you and talk as one human does to another.'

I felt someone come and sit by the mosquito net around me. Sensing that there would be no sleep for me, I said with an air of eagerness, 'Capital! Tell me a story that makes me happy.'

'If you want to hear something truly entertaining, let me tell you about my own life,' it said.

The church bells struck two.

'When I was human and still a child, there was one person that I feared like death itself. That was my husband. I felt just like a fish caught on a hook. As if a complete stranger had hauled me from the gentle familiarity of my home, with a sharp pull and with no hope of escape. He died two months after our marriage and all my relatives wept copiously on my behalf. My father-in-law looked at many of my features and said to my mother-in-law, "This is a woman of ill omen." I remember this clearly—are you listening? How do you find it so far?'

I replied, 'Good. You have started well.'

'Then listen on; I returned to my own home happily. As the years passed, I grew older. People tried to hide it from me, but I knew that without a doubt it was hard to find someone as beautiful as me. What do you feel?'

'Possibly; But then I have never seen you.'

'Have you not? Why, what about that skeleton? But I jest. How can I prove to you that there were once a pair of dark luminous eyes within these bony eye sockets and that the gentle smile that softened my red lips has no comparison in today's lipless grimace; or that it makes me both laugh and cry to tell you about the beauty and grace that wrapped about these dry bones and the youthful perfection that grew to fruition in my body. Not even the best doctors of the time would have believed that this exquisite form would have provided lessons in the names of bones one day. I have heard that one doctor of my time described me as a magnolia blossom to one of his close friends. He meant that all others might have been repositories for bones and physiology, but I was as beautiful as a flower. Does a flower need a skeleton?

'When I walked I knew that every movement I made was beautiful and the sway of my body spread natural happiness wherever I went, just as a diamond sparkles when it is moved. I sometimes spent a long time looking at my own hand—knowing that they could have reined in all the arrogance of the men on earth. I suppose Subhadra must have had hands like that when she rode away with Arjuna on her own chariot through the three worlds. Just such a pair of slender arms, the same blush suffused palms and fingers that glowed like flames of beauty.

'But that shamelessly naked and eternally ancient skeleton is a false witness to my name. I remained mute and unable to answer at the time. That is why my greatest grievances are against you. I wish I could bring that living, breathing, sixteen-year-old, filled as she was with the pride of youth, to stand before your eyes once and drive the sleep from your eyes for a good many days; drive those names of bones that still rattle around in your skull away for good.'

I said, 'If you were alive, I would swear upon your life and tell you that I remember nothing of those names of bones. The beauty that was once yours and famed through the world is still burning bright in the darkness. You do not have to say any more.'

'I had no female companions of my own. My brother had pledged to never marry. I was alone in the house and I would sit in the garden under a tree and think that the whole world was adoring me, all the stars were looking upon me, the breeze was finding an excuse to pass by me with sighs and the grass that lay under my feet would pass out if only it had known who I was. I imagined the blades of grass to be like the young men of the planet, all congregated at my feet, and the pain of something hurt my heart.

'When my elder brother's friend Shashisekhar passed out of Medical College, he became our family physician. I had often observed him secretly. My brother was a very unusual person who seemed not to notice his surroundings. It was as though life was not solitary enough for him; he took refuge at its furthest corner.

'Shashisekhar was one of his friends. That is how we met often. That is why when I sat like an empress under the flowering tree each evening, he represented the entire race of men at my feet. Are you listening? What do you feel?'

I said with a sigh, 'I think it would have been good to be born as Shashisekhar.'

'Listen to my entire story first. One rainy evening, I had a fever and the doctor was summoned. That was the first time we met.'

'I was lying with my face to the window, so that the red glow of the evening fell on my face and brightened my pale visage. When he came into the room and looked at me, I tried to imagine myself as the doctor looking upon me.

'The evening light fell upon a slightly pained face that lay like a flower upon the soft pillows; the untamed curls fell upon the forehead of that face and lashes shaded the cheeks, as the luminous eyes looked downwards shyly.

'The doctor said softly in a low voice to my brother, "The pulse needs to be checked once."'

'I freed my shapely arm from the covers that sheltered its weariness. As I did so, I looked at my hand and thought that it would have been well if I had worn blue glass at the wrists. I have never seen a doctor hesitate for so long before checking a patient's pulse. He checked it with shaking fingers and very unmindfully. He felt my fever and I understood something of the pulse of the storm within his soul. Do you not believe me?'

I answered, 'I see no reason for disbelief—a pulse is prone to behaving oddly.'

'After a few more illnesses and convalescing, I found that the number of men at my feet diminished to only one and my world became emptier and emptier. The only two people in that world were a doctor and his patient.

'I would secretly wear a golden yellow saree, do my hair with jasmine blossoms and sit in the garden with a mirror in the evenings.

'Why? Was I not satisfied with seeing myself? Not really. Because I did not see me then; I became two people each time I was alone. I looked upon myself through the doctor's eyes, delighting in myself and loving and adoring myself while a sigh rose within my soul like an evening breeze.

'I was never alone from that day onwards; when I walked I watched my toes caressing the ground and thought about how the doctor felt when he heard them; when the midday sun blazed outside my window and there was no one about except for a kite calling in the distant skies; when the toy-seller walked outside our garden walls calling out "Who wants toys, who will buy my bangles?", I would spread a spotless sheet on my bed and casually place a bare arm on its softness, thinking of someone looking at the arm, someone raising it in their own hands, someone kissing my blushing palm and leaving slowly.—What if my story ended here? How would that be?'

I said, 'It would not be bad at all. Perhaps a little unfinished but I can imagine an ending for myself through the remainder of this night.'

'But then the story ends up being far too sombre. Where is the trick in this? How do you know why the skeleton smiles so broadly?'

'Listen to the rest of it. As soon as his name spread a little, the doctor opened a chamber on the ground floor of our house. I used to tease him a little, asking him all about drugs that healed and those that killed and how people could take lives easily. He would answer any medical questions without hesitation. Thus death became something I began to see as a friend; love and death became the only two realities of life.'

'My story is almost done, there is very little of it left.'

I said softly, 'There is very little left of this night too.'

'I had noticed that the doctor was growing absentminded lately and seemed ill at ease in my presence. One day I saw him come to our house rather more richly dressed than usual and ask to borrow my brother's carriage for some evening engagement.'

'I could not be silent any longer. I went to my brother and after talking about a few other things I asked, "Where is the doctor going tonight with the carriage?"'

'My brother answered briefly, "To his death."'

'No, please tell me the truth,' I insisted.

'He answered in a little more detail this time and said, "To get married."

'"Really?" I said and laughed for long.'

'I gradually found out that the doctor was to receive a dowry of twelve thousand rupees from this marriage. But why insult me by concealing this from me? Had I entreated him to not do this as I would surely die, if he did? Who can believe a man's word? I saw but one man in my entire life and that was enough for me.'

'When he came to the room before evening fell after seeing the sick, I laughed at my own humour and asked, "What is this I hear? Apparently you are to marry tonight?"

'Not only was he uncomfortable at my mirth, he seemed to be saddened as well.'

'I asked, "Where are the musicians?"'

'He said with a sigh, "Is a marriage that happy an occasion?"

'I nearly died laughing at that. I had never heard someone say such a thing before. I said, "No, that cannot be! There must be music and lots of lights!"

'I pressed my brother so much that he went to get the musicians and the lights organised.

'I talked endlessly of what we would do when the new bride arrived. I asked, "Now tell me, doctor, will you still check people's pulses then?"

'Although one cannot see the mind, especially in men, I can swear that the words pierced him like an arrow.

'His marriage was to be held very late at night. Like the other evenings, the doctor was sitting on the roof terrace having a drink with my brother. The moon rose gradually in the sky.

'I arrived with smiles wreathing my face and asked, "Have you forgotten that it is time to go, Doctor?"

'I might have to tell you a little secret here. I had secretly gone to his rooms earlier and had stolen some powders. I added some of it to the doctor's glass, when no one was watching me.

'From him I had already learned which of his powders killed people.

'The doctor finished his glass hurriedly and looked at me with abject misery as he said, "I must leave now."

'The flute played on and I wore a saree of silk and brocade. I put on all the jewellery I had in my chest and drew a line of vermilion through my parting. I made a bed at the base of my favourite mimosa tree.

'It was a beautiful night with bright moonlight all around. The southern breeze was blowing, taking with it all the weariness of the sleeping world. The entire garden was filled with the perfume rising from the blooming jasmine.

'When the sound of the flute faded into the distance and the moonlight gave way to darkness, when the earth with its trees, the sky and the familiar surroundings of home began to fade away, I closed my eyes and smiled.

'I had hoped that this smile would always touch my lips with seductive charm when people came and looked at me. I had hoped to take this smile along with me when I joined the eternal. But nothing like that happened! When I woke to a dry clacking, I found three young boys learning the names of my bones. Their tutor pointed with a cane right at my ribs—where sorrows and happiness once pulsed and the petals of youth once unfurled one by one—and talked about the names of bones! Did you see any sign of the smile that had graced my lips at that final moment?

'What did you think about the story?'

I replied, 'It is quite amusing.'

The first crow of the morning called. I asked, 'Are you still here?'

There was no answer.

The light of dawn entered the room.

(Konkal – Golpo Guchcho)

Hungry Stones

We met the gentleman on the train while my relative and I were returning to Kolkata after our holidays. At first, when I saw his clothes I thought he was a Muslim gentleman from the west. My confusion increased when I heard him speak. He had so much to say about each and every thing on earth, it was as though the Creator did everything after discussing it with him first. We had been completely at peace thanks to our ignorance about many unheard of secrets; the advance of the Russians, the secret plans of the English and the tangled intrigues of the Indian princes. Our newfound acquaintance smiled slightly and said, 'There happen more things in heaven and earth, Horatio, than are reported in your newspapers.' This was the first time we had left our homes and this man's strange behavior surprised us. At the slightest excuse, he talked about science, quoted the Vedas

and recited Farsi couplets. As we had no knowledge of science, the Vedas or Farsi our reverence for him grew progressively. Even my theosophist relative started believing that this co-traveller of ours had some kind of supernatural aura; a kind of astonishing magnetism if you will, or unearthly power, or paranormal abilities or something of a similar nature. He was listening to everything this extraordinary man said with awestruck reverence and was making secret notes; I felt that the extraordinary man had understood this too and was enjoying it.

When the train stopped at the junction, we bided our time as a group in the waiting room. It was half past ten at night. We heard that the train was quite delayed due to problems on the route. I had already decided to spread out my bed roll and sleep on a table when the extraordinary gentleman started to tell us the following story. Needless to say, I did not get any sleep at all for the rest of that night.

When I resigned my position at Junagadh after a few disagreements regarding how the kingdom should be run and joined the Nizam's government at Hyderabad, seeing that I was a hardy young man, they posted me at Barich as a cotton tax collector.

Barich was a very pleasant place. The Shusta (from the original Swachchatoya in Sanskrit) flowed fast over a pebbled bed, like the swaying motion of an expert dancer through great forests at the feet of lonely peaks. From the river, a hundred and fifty marble steps led to a palace made of white stone that stood alone at the base of the mountains—there were no other houses nearby. The cotton market at Barich and the village were far from here.

Shah Mahmud the Second had built his palace for pleasure in this remote place, almost two-hundred-and-fifty years ago. From then on, rose-scented water flowed in fountains from the bathing houses and young Persian beauties sat, hair flowing down their backs, with their pretty bare feet in the clear waters of the pool's stone seats in those secret rooms, with their sitars across their laps and singing songs of the grape arbour of their native lands.

Those fountains do not flow any more, those songs no longer fill the air, nor do those fair feet fall upon the white stone floors—today it is a vast and terribly empty dwelling for tax collectors like me, deprived of female company and oppressed by the loneliness of our surroundings. But the ancient clerk at work, Karim Khan, had cautioned me repeatedly against staying there, saying to me, 'stay here if you must during the day, but never spend the night here.' I laughed his worries off. The servants said they would work till evening but they too refused to stay at night. I said, 'So be it.' The house was so infamous that even thieves refused to try their luck at night.

Initially, the emptiness of the abandoned palace used to weigh on me like a terrible weight. I used to try and stay away for as long as possible and work continually, only to return home exhausted and fall sleep.

But within a week, the house began to encompass me with a strange spell. It would be hard to describe my state and even to make people believe me. The entire house started to absorb me, like a living thing being drawn slowly into a digestive system.

Possibly this process had started the moment I set foot in the house—but I still remember the day I first noticed its beginnings within my consciousness.

The market was slow at the start of summer and I had no work to do. I was sitting on an easy chair at the bottom of those steps, one evening a little before sunset. The river had grown shallow over summer; a large part of the sandy banks on the opposite side were coloured by the rays of the setting sun. On this shore, the pebbles could be seen glinting in the shallow waters of the river hugging the steps. There was not even a whisper of a breeze anywhere. A dense perfume rose from the wild basil, mint and fennel forests of the nearby mountains and filled the still skies with aromatic heaviness.

When the sun descended behind the shelter of the peaks, a curtain of shadow immediately fell across the arena of the day—the mountains here prevent the mingling of light and dark from lasting long at sunset. I was thinking of going for a ride on my horse when I suddenly heard footsteps on the stairs. When I looked back, there was no one present.

Thinking it to be a trick of my senses, I turned my back once again; immediately I heard the sounds of a number of feet, as though many people were running down the stairs. My whole body trembled with the most delicious thrill, mixed with a slight degree of fear. Even though there was nothing before me, I felt as though I could clearly see a group of vivacious women descending into the river to bathe. Although there were no sounds to be heard anywhere that evening—either on the silent mountain slopes or in the deserted palace on that river bank—I could still clearly hear the bathers chase each other past me with peals of amused laughter like the hundred streams of a waterfall. They did not seem to notice me. Just as they were invisible to me, I was invisible to them. The river was just as peaceful as before, but I clearly felt the shallow water being churned by the movements of many bangle-bedecked arms; they were splashing each other with water as they laughed and the water droplets flew like hands full of pearls into the sky as the swimmers playfully kicked their legs in the river.

There was a trembling in my heart; I cannot say whether that thrill was caused by fear, joy or curiosity. I greatly wished to see them better, but there was nothing to see; it felt like I would be able to hear everything clearly if I only tried harder—but when I did, I could only hear the crickets in the forest. It was as though a two-hundred-and-fifty year old black curtain was hanging in front of me—I had fearfully raised a corner and peeped in—there was a great gathering within but I could see nothing in the dense darkness.

Suddenly the stillness was broken by a breeze— the flat river surface rippled like waves in the hair of some celestial dancer and the entire forest shook itself free from a nightmare with a great murmur. Whether it was a dream or the real thing, the invisible mirage that had appeared before me from two-hundred-and-fifty years ago disappeared in the blink of an eye. The enchantresses who had pushed past me on ghostly steps with noiseless laughter to leap into the Shusta no longer walked past me as they returned from their baths in their wet clothes. Just as the wind blows perfume away, they disappeared with one whisper from the spring breeze.

I then felt very worried that aided by the solitude that surrounded the place, the muse of poetry had taken up with me; I was a hard-working tax collector, what would happen to me now? I decided that I needed to eat properly; an empty stomach was known to be the root of many a difficult disease. I summoned my cook and ordered him to prepare many rich dishes redolent with ghee and spices.

The next morning it all seemed very laughable. I happily dressed like a Westerner in a sola topee, called for a carriage myself and went to work with the loud grinding of wheels. I was supposed to be late going home, late as I had to write a tri-monthly report. But as soon as dusk fell, I felt drawn to my home. I did not know who was calling me, but I felt that I could not delay going home any longer. I felt as though everyone was waiting for me. Leaving that report incomplete, I put my topee on and went home to that darkened, silent, vast mountain mansion, startling the lonely, tree-shaded dusk-blurred road with the sound of carriage wheels.

The room facing the stairs was vast indeed. Three rows of enormous columns topped with ornate beams held up the roof. This huge room used to vibrate under the weight of its own emptiness day and night. No lamps had been lit that evening. As soon as I entered that room, pushing the door open, it seemed as though a great uproar broke out—a great throng of people left the place suddenly in a hurry through all the doors and windows around the room. I stood in astonishment as I could not see anything. My body thrilled to a strange feeling. I could almost smell the traces of long gone perfumes and hair oils.

I stood in that great dark empty space surrounded by those ancient stone pillars and heard—the splashing of water from fountains on to white stone, a tune that I did not recognise being plucked on the sitar, from somewhere came the tinkle of golden ornaments, from other rooms came the sounds of anklets and the occasional clang of massive copper bells to mark the time; the keening of flutes from a great distance, the silvery clinking of the crystal pendants of the chandeliers as the wind blew threw them, trills from caged bulbuls on the verandah, the harsher cries of tame water birds from the garden further away—all these created a ghostly symphony all around me.

I felt so entranced; it felt as though this intangible, unattainable and unreal world was the only truth, and all else mere mirages. Facts such as my name, that I was my father's eldest son, that I earned four hundred and fifty rupees as a cotton tax collector and went to work in hat and coat by carriage, all these seemed so incredibly laughable to me that I stood in the middle of that vast silent darkness and laughed aloud at the baseless lies that they were.

At that very moment my Muslim household help came into the room with a lighted kerosene lamp. I do not know whether he thought me mad but I immediately remembered that I was after all my father's eldest son; I also thought that even if somewhere in this world or without, a ghostly fountain was bubbling for eternity and unseen fingers were plucking tunes on ethereal strings, it was up to the great poets to say such things. For me the only truth was that I got paid four hundred and fifty rupees for collecting taxes on cotton sold in the market at Barich. I thought of the trance of a while ago and smiled with amusement as I sat close to the kerosene-illuminated camp table to read my newspaper.

After reading the paper and eating the Mughlai food, I went to one of the tiny rooms at the back of the house and lay down on the bed. Through the open window before me, a very bright star burned millions of miles away above the dark forested peaks of the Arali ranges, looking down at a tax collector reclining on a lowly camp bed; as I thought about it with both wonder and amusement. I fell asleep at one point. I do not know for how long I had slept. I woke with a sudden start. There had not been any sound in the room, and neither did I see anyone come in. The watchful star had set behind the dark mountain and the wan moonlight had hesitantly crept in through the window.

I saw no one at all. Yet I felt certain that someone was gently nudging me. As soon as I woke, she wordlessly beckoned with her be-ringed hand to follow her.

I got up very quietly. In spite of there being not a single other person in that hundred-roomed palace filled with the weight of a vast emptiness, the sounds of silence and alertly awaiting echoes, I still felt fear dog each footstep lest I woke someone. Most of the rooms were closed and I had never been inside them.

Today I could not say where I walked, as I followed the call of that unseen vision on silent footsteps and silenced breaths. I passed through many narrow darkened passages, wide verandahs, great halls that stood sombre with silent expectation and airless hidden rooms with terrible secrets of their own.

Even though I had not seen the invisible messenger, her form was not unknown to me. She was an Arab beauty, her shapely fair alabaster arms visible through her loose sleeves, a veil hanging over her face from a cap perched on her head and a curved scimitar at her waist.

I felt as though one of the thousand and one nights of the famed Arabian tales had arrived in my life. I was walking the unlit streets of Baghdad in a tryst with something fearful on that dark night.

Eventually, my guide stopped suddenly before a curtain that was of the darkest blue and pointed at something below. There was nothing there but my very blood seemed to freeze in terror. I sensed that there was a terrifying eunuch guard who nodded in slumber, an unsheathed sword on his lap in readiness. She stepped lightly over his legs and lifted an end of the drapes.

A part of a room spread with rich Persian carpets could be seen. I could not see the person sitting on the throne but a pair of tiny delicate feet in brocade slippers peeped out from the ends of flowing pants of a saffron colour. These rested idly on a foot stool covered in pink velvet. By the side sat a bluish crystal bowl of apples, pears, oranges and many bunches of grapes and two small cups stood with a golden wine-filled carafe, next to the fruits. Smoke from some wondrous incense burning within the room filled the air and intoxicated my senses as I breathed it in.

Trembling, I tried to step over the sleeping guard's feet but he immediately woke up—the sword falling from his hands with a clatter.

Suddenly a horrific shout startled me and I woke abruptly to see myself sitting in a sweat on the camp bed, with dawn light rendering the moon as pale as a sleepless convalescent—and outside Meher Ali the Mad carrying out his morning routine of shouting, 'Keep away! Keep away!' on the empty roads of the early hours.

This is how the first of my Arabian fairy tale nights ended, but there were still a thousand more to endure.

My nights and my days grew very conflicted. I would go to work exhausted and curse my nights of illusion and empty dreams; as darkness fell, my hours at work became an insignificant lie and quite laughable in the scheme of things.

I would find myself entangled in a web of obsessive yearning as soon as evening fell. I became part of that unwritten story of centuries ago; no longer did the suits of the foreigner and the tailored trousers seem the right attire. Instead, I found myself dressing with great care, selecting a red velvet fez for my head, loose pants, flowery over shirts and long silken coats, an attar-soaked colourful kerchief twisted between my fingers as I put aside my cigarettes and smoked from an enormous hookah filled with rose water, sitting in a cushioned chair. One might say, I was waiting eagerly for the arrival of someone very dear to me.

I find it impossible to describe the strange turn of events as darkness grew. It was as if tableaus from a wonderful tale were blown into this time by a spring breeze and were now floating about the various rooms of the huge mansion. One could follow the story for a while but not beyond that. I did just that all night through the rooms.

Every now and again a woman would appear within these vignettes swirling within the fragmented dreams, sometimes in a whiff of henna, sometimes in a tinkle of the sitar and in a sudden delight of scented mist. She was the one who wore the saffron pyjamas and a pair of curved brocade shoes encasing her two fair feet. She wore a flowered brocade bodice, a red cap on her head and a golden veil that descended from the cap to conceal and cover her fair forehead and her cheeks.

She had intoxicated me. I wandered the alleys and depths of that hellish kingdom each night in search of her through the dangerous twisted paths of palaces, peopled with nightmares.

Some days, as I stood in front of the huge mirror with lights on either side of me, dressing myself as a prince, I would see that young Iranian woman reflected in the mirror next to me—in a trice she would turn away, after casting an eager expressive passionate look at me from her huge dark eyes and whispering a hint of some words; she would spin on her heel, raising waves of pain, desire and enchantment before disappearing within the mirror, leaving behind traces of the brilliance of her smile and her jewels. A sudden wind carrying all the scents stolen from the gardens and groves of the surrounding mountains would suddenly put out both my lights. I would stop dressing and lie down on the bed adjoining the dressing area, my body thrilled by her presence, my eyes closed, listening to the winds bring memories of kisses and loving touches that swirled through the room in the dark. I would hear the murmur of many voices, someone would breathe sweetly on my forehead and a perfumed soft veil would trail deliciously across my cheeks again and again. I would slowly be entrapped in the enchanting embrace of a seductive serpent, my breath falling rapidly until I surrendered my unfeeling body to a deep sleep.

One afternoon I decided to take a ride on the horse—I felt someone restraining me but that day I paid no heed. My Western hat and shirt were hanging on a wooden stand; as I prepared to put them on, a great wind rose in eddies of river sand and dry leaves from the Arali Mountains and carried the hat spinning into the distance. A sweet tinkling laugh spun around me with the breeze, touching on every note of amusement till it faded away in the light of the setting sun.

I did not ride my horse that day and completely gave up wearing the ridiculous shirt and hat from the next day.

At midnight again, I sat up in my bed and heard someone sobbing plaintively as if her heart would break—under my very bed, under the floor, deep from within a wet dark grave under the very stone foundations of this vast palace, crying to me—'save me, take me away—leaving harsh illusion, deep sleep, broken dreams—all these behind, place me on your horse, clasp me to your breast and carry me away through forests and over mountain peaks, across rivers; take me to the sunlight of your rooms. Save me!'

Who was I! How was I to rescue anyone? Which drowning siren of desire would I pull out from this revolving, ever-changing whirlpool of dreams! When did you exist? Where were you, formless one? Where did you take birth, under the shade of date palms by which cool streams in the lap of what wandering desert dweller? What Bedouin bandit stole you from her lap like a bud torn from a wild vine, and rushed on horses with lightning fast hooves across burning sands to sell you at the slave marts of what exotic capital? There a trusted servant of the Padishah must have examined the newly blossoming shy beauty of your youth and counted out golden coins, placed you on a ship and then finally in a golden palanquin to be presented to his master. The history there! The strains of the sarengi, the tinkling of anklets and the liquid gold in the wine cups must be marred by flashing knives, poisoned chalices and hateful glances. What endless wealth, what eternal imprisonment. Two slave girls flash diamonds at their wrists as they fan the emperor, jewel encrusted shoes scattered at his feet. Outside an Abyssinian as fearsome as a messenger of death but dressed like a heavenly messenger in borrowed finery, stands guard with an open blade. After swirling about on that bloody, spite-flecked web of deceit and ugly wealth, a flower of the desert ends up, saved from cruel death or perhaps cast upon the shores of an even cruel fate.

Suddenly Meher Ali, the madman shouted, 'Stay away, stay away, it is all lies, all lies!' I opened my eyes and saw that dawn had broken; my valet gave me the mail and the chef came and asked what he was to prepare that day.

I said, no, I cannot stay here anymore. I took all my belongings to the office. The old clerk Karim Khan smiled slightly on seeing me. I was annoyed by his smile and kept working wordlessly.

As the afternoon approached, I found myself growing distracted. I kept thinking I had to go somewhere, the work of calculating cotton sales seemed to be completely unnecessary. My existence in the Nizam's employ, the pay, the present that surrounded me, the moving, living, breathing world around me seemed impoverished, meaningless and unnecessary.

I threw my pen down, shut the huge ledger and ran to the carriage. It stopped at the doors to that stone palace just as the twilight hour was upon us. I climbed the steps fast and went into the house.

Today all was quiet. The darkened rooms seemed to be brooding in anger. My heart heaved in repentance, but who would hear my entreaties? I found no one I could beg forgiveness from. I wandered through the rooms, my mind emptied of all thought. I felt like singing to someone, felt like saying, 'Fire, the moth that sought to escape you has returned to embrace death. Now forgive it, singe its wings, burn it to nothingness.'

Suddenly two tears fell on my forehead from above. Dense clouds had wreathed the peaks of the Arali Mountains that day. The dark forests and the inky depths of the river seemed silenced in a terrible wait. Everything trembled and suddenly a storm rushed at us, baring teeth of lightning, like a mad man freed from his shackles with screams of terror through the pathless depths of distant forests. The doors to the vast un-peopled rooms of the palace banged in the wind as if in intense pain.

Today all the servants were in the office and no one had been there to light the lamps. In the pitch black darkness of that cloudy moonless night I could clearly feel that—a woman was lying prostrate on the carpet at the foot of the bed; her long hair coming away in her angry fists as she pulled at it, her fair forehead bleeding from a cut. Now she would laugh, a shrill mirthless sound, and then suddenly her whole body would be wracked with sobs. She struck at her bosom as she ripped away her blouse and the wind roared in through the open window as the rain rushed in and drenched her whole body.

The storm and the weeping went on that whole night. I wandered the rooms in the darkness in fruitless lament. There was no one else there that I could console. Whose was this great anger? Where was this restless repentance coming from?

The mad man cried out, 'Keep your distance! Keep your distance! They are all lies! They are all lies!'

I found it was already dawn and Meher Ali had done his usual walk around the palace and was now shouting his usual phrases despite the storm. I suddenly thought that he too might have once lived in the palace, even after succumbing to lunacy and while leaving, he was still caught up in the spell cast by the demon stones and came to circle around the place each morning.

I immediately ran to him in the rain and asked him, 'Meher Ali, what lies are these?'

He did not reply and pushed past me calling frantically, like a bird in the thrall of a python's coils, on his path around the house. He kept crying out that warning to himself, 'Keep your distance, keep your distance! They are all lies! They are all lies!'

Like one possessed, I rushed to the office in that storm and asked Karim Khan, 'Tell me what all this means!'

What the old man said was this: once the palace had been the scene of many unsatisfied desires and much untamed passion—whose anguished souls and unrequited lust had cursed each and every stone with an eternal hunger; they seized upon living men and devoured them when they could. Of all the people to live in that palace, only Meher Ali had survived, although he had become insane. The rest had never been seen again.

'Is there no way then of saving me?' I asked.

'There is a way', said the old man, 'But it is very difficult. I will tell you but first let me share with you the story of an Iranian slave girl in Gulbag. Nothing quite as amazing and tragic has ever taken place on this earth.'

> The porters came and told us that the train was coming. So soon? As we quickly packed our things again, the train arrived. An Englishman who must have just woken up looked out of a window of the First Class carriage to read the name of the station, saw our co-passenger and greeted him loudly before inviting him into his own compartment. We boarded the Second Class carriage. We did not get to know who he was, nor did we hear the end of the story.
>
> I declared that the man had amused himself at our expense because he saw we were clearly quite inexperienced; his story was completely made up.
>
> This led to an argument that ended my friendship with the theosophist.

(Khudhito Pashaan – Golpo Guchcho)

Ramkanai's Folly

Those who say Gurucharan's second wife was playing cards in her own quarters while her husband lay on his deathbed are a slanderous bunch making mountains out of molehills. In actual fact, she was sitting down with one leg tucked underneath and the other knee drawn up to her chest, eating some day-old rice that she had mixed with green tamarind, chillies and a spicy prawn curry. When the call came from the sickroom, she pushed the mound of chewed vegetables and the empty plate away and said sombrely, 'I do not even have the time to eat a few morsels of stale rice!'

When the doctor left saying there was nothing more that he could do, Gurucharan's brother Ramkanai sat down beside him and said softly, 'If you wish to make a will tell me so.' Gurucharan said weakly, 'I will speak, please write everything down.' Ramkanai gathered pen and paper as Gurucharan started saying, 'I leave all my moveable and immoveable property to my lawfully wedded wife Borodashundori.' Ramkanai did write this down but his pen seemed to take forever. He had hoped so very much that his only child Nabadwip would inherit the entire estate of this childless uncle. Even though the two brothers had separate kitchens, Ramkanai's wife had prevented her son from taking up any gainful employment in this hope and had married him off rather early. To the dismay of their enemies, the marriage had also been fruitful. But he still wrote everything down faithfully and handed the pen to his elder brother for his signature. Gurucharan's scribble was so faint that it was hard to understand whether it was his name or a few shaky lines on paper.

When his wife did appear after finishing her meal, he was no longer able to say anything and his wife started weeping. All the people who had greatly wished for a windfall for themselves said that she was pretending, but that is not true.

When Nabadwip's mother heard of the will, she arrived in a greatly incensed state and created an uproar saying, 'People lose their senses when death approaches. Why else would he ignore such a deserving nephew?'

Even though Ramkanai respected his wife excessively—to the extent that it could be described as fear—he could not ignore this. He swiftly stepped in and said, 'This is not the time for you to lose your senses; why are you behaving this way? He is dead, but I am here. If you have something to say, say it to me later for now is not the time for this.'

When Nabadwip heard the news, he came to find that his uncle had already passed away. He angrily threatened him nonetheless and said, 'I will see who performs the funeral rites! If you expect me to do them, you are greatly mistaken.'

Gurucharan had never believed in any of these things. He had been a student of Mr Duff's. He took great enjoyment in doing the things described as taboo in the Scriptures. If people called him a Christian, he shook his head and said, 'Then I must eat beef.' The person who had been like this all his life could hardly be expected to be disturbed by threats to the funeral ceremony, now that he was newly dead. But there was no other way of taking revenge on him. Nabadwip was mollified by the realisation that his uncle would never come back to life again. Even without his uncle's money he would be able to subsist for the rest of his days, but his uncle was now in such a place where one could not find a chance at living even if one begged for it. There is much to be said about being alive.

Ramkanai went to Borodashundori and said to her, 'Sister-in-law, my brother has left everything to you. This is his will. Lock it away carefully in your iron chest.'

The widow was busy wailing, making up new phrases to express her sorrow as she went along and a couple of the maids had joined in and added a few words of their own; between them they were successfully keeping the entire neighbourhood awake. The arrival of the piece of paper that Ramkanai was giving her caused a break in the pattern and led to the disjointed events described below:

'Alas, what misfortune, what a terrible thing this is for me. Okay brother-in-law, whose handwriting is this? Yours? Alas, who will look after me with that kind of attention, who will look at me at all! Can you people be quiet, don't shriek so much, let me hear his words. Alas, why did I not get taken first? Why am I still alive!' Ramkanai thought quietly, 'That is indeed our misfortune.'

When he went home, his wife started on him. Ramkanai stood silent for a long time, putting up with all of it much as a bullock will steadfastly stand after slipping into a ditch with an overloaded cart, no matter how much the driver pokes him. Finally, he said in a pained voice, 'How is any of this my fault? I am not the one who made the will.'

Nabadwip's mother hissed at him, 'No, of course not, you are such a good man, you don't understand what you have done; your brother said write this down, and you wrote it down straight away. You are all the same! You must be waiting for your turn to be able to do the same. The minute I die you will marry some horrible witch and bring her home—and cast out my darling Nabadwip. But don't worry! I am not going to die any time soon.'

She grew more and more annoyed as she discussed this future misbehaviour. Ramkanai knew for certain that if he said anything to assure her against these outlandish and imagined fears, it would only get worse. Hence he stood there looking guilty, as though the deed had already been done and he had died and deprived 'darling Nabadwip', giving everything to his second wife! There was nothing to do but admit to the offence.

In the meantime, Nabadwip consulted his clever friends and came to his mother saying, 'There is nothing to worry about. I will have it all. We have to send my father somewhere else for a few days. If he stays, things will not work out.' His mother had no respect for his father's sense either and this seemed a logical thing to do. In a few days, this extremely unnecessary, foolish, obstinate man was packed off to Kashi for a few days, on some excuse.

Within a short while Borodashundori and Nabadwip Chandra had gone to court, after accusing each other of forging the will. Nabadwip had produced a will in his favour where Gurucharan's name was clearly written in his own hand and—he even had a couple of unbiased witnesses. Borodashundori's only witness was Nabadwip's father and there was no way of reading the signature on the will she had. She had a cousin living in their house who said, 'Sister, never fear, I will be your witness and I will find others to bear witness for you.'

When the situation was completely muddled up, Nabadwip's mother sent for his father. The devoted gentleman came with his bag and his umbrella. He even tried out some humour, saying with folded hands, 'The knave is here! What does the queen wish me to do?'

She shook her head and said, 'Enough of these lies. I am sure you never thought of me when you were in Kashi all this time.'

The two continued to trade playful insults for a long time. Gradually the insults became complaints that were directed against the other's gender, rather than the individual. Nabadwip's mother compared the love in the hearts of men with the love of a Mussalman for chicken*. Nabadwip's father said, 'Women have honey on their lips but blades in their hearts'—although it is hard to say when, if ever, he had received proof of these honeyed words.

Ramkanai received a subpoena from the court, asking him to stand witness. While he was trying to comprehend this, Nabadwip's mother came to him in a flood of tears saying, 'That witch is not just trying to deprive my dear Nabadwip from rightfully inheriting his loving uncle's property, she is now working on sending him to jail.'

Eventually, when he understood the entire affair, Ramkanai was appalled. He shouted, 'What have you done!' His wife adopted her usual attitude and asked, 'Why, how is this Nabadwip's fault in any way? Why should he not inherit his uncle's property! Why should he let it go!' takes it all? If a foolish What good-natured, deserving descendant can bear it when a rapacious, husband-eating, daughter of evil comes out of nowhere and uncle loses his mind, thanks to the twin effects of death and the spells of said witch, then why is it wrong for the blameless nephew to try and correct the wrongs himself?

Ramkanai was astounded to see that his wife and son had joined forces in alternately berating him; he struck his forehead in shame as he wept, refusing to eat or even drink water.

After two days had passed in this silent abstinence from food and drink, it was time for the trial. Nabadwip had managed to convince and arm twist Borodashundori's cousin with promises and threats into giving witness in his favour. When victory was about to abandon Borodashundori's camp and move to the other side, Ramkanai was summoned to the witness stand.

Weakened by hunger, the old man gripped the stand with his trembling thin fingers, his lips and tongue dry, as though he faced the gallows. The cunning barrister began his questioning in an attempt to find out the truth—starting from afar and proceeding to reel his prey in with great care.

Ramkanai then turned to the judge and said respectfully, 'My lord, I am old and very weak. I do not have the strength to say a lot. Let me tell you what I know. My brother, the late Gurucharan Chakravarti, left all his property to his wife Madam Borodashundori by legal will at the time of his death. I wrote it out and he signed it with his own hand. The will that my son Nabadwip Chandra has submitted to this court is false.' After saying these words, he fainted.

Amused, the clever barrister said to the attorney beside him, 'By Jove! How well did I corner the fellow!' The cousin ran to his sister and said, 'The old man was about to ruin the case, but thanks to my statement, the tide is turning.'

The sister said, 'Really? I always thought of him as a good man!'

The clever friends of the imprisoned Nabadwip decided after much discussion that the old man must have been frightened into doing such a thing, or that he had lost his head in the witness stand; a more utterly foolish man would be hard to find in the city.

When he came home, Ramkanai became feverish. Soon this stupid, unnecessary, man who had managed to ruin all the plans of others died, calling for his son in his delirious state.

Some of his relatives said, 'It would have been best if he had gone and died a few days earlier.' But I do not wish to name any names or say who these were.

(Ramkanai-er Nirbuddhita – Golpo Guchcho)

The Jewels

My boat was moored at the edge of a dilapidated jetty. The sun had already set and the boatman was offering his evening prayers on the roof of the boat. His silent prayers were expressed as an ever-changing tableau in the red-gold of the western sky. The still, unmarked surface of the river reflected an indescribable spectrum of colours from pale to bold, from sunset gold to the steel grey of night, one shade merging with another.

As I was about to fall under the spell of the song of the cicadas that heralded that sunset sky in addition to the brooding presence of an ancient decaying mansion nearby, growing slightly moist-eyed at its broken windows and collapsed balconies which were adding to the already depressing surrounds of the jetty, half strangled as it was by tree roots, I started suddenly at the sound of someone saying, 'And where might you be coming from?'

I saw that the speaker was an emaciated, unfortunate-looking individual. He looked like many of my countrymen abroad, as though he had been in need of rejuvenation for a long time. He was dressed in a dhoti and a grimy unbuttoned top made of Assamese raw silk that made him look like he had just returned from work. He seemed to have come to sample the evening breeze at the river's edge rather than stay home and have the meal that he should have been enjoying, given the hour.

The newcomer sat on the steps to one side.

'I have come from Ranchi,' I said.

'What do you do?'

'I am in business.'

'What kind of business?'

'I deal in myrobalan, silk cocoons and wood.'

'What is your name?'

I paused slightly before giving him a name that was not my own.

His curiosity was still unsatisfied. He asked again, 'Why are you here?'

I replied, 'For a change of scenery.'

The fellow was slightly astonished. He said, 'Dear Sir, I have been savouring the change of scenery here for the past six years along with fifteen grains of quinine each day, but I am yet to see any change in myself!'

I said, 'The scenery is bound to be different from Ranchi.'

'That is true. Where are you staying here?' he queried.

I indicated the old house above the bank and said, 'Over there.'

I think he was suspicious that I had found some hidden treasure in the old house. But instead of asking me about that, he described the events that took place fifteen years ago in that cursed mansion in some detail.

The man was the local school master. His prominent eyes burned unnaturally bright in the sunken depths of his famished and sickly face. His head was large and hairless. He reminded me of Coleridge's Ancient Mariner.

The boatmen had started to cook their evening meals after their prayers. The last of the evening light had faded and the empty house loomed in the darkness like a huge ghostly reminder of its past.

The school master continued with his story:

Ten years before I came to the village, Phanibhushan Saha used to live in this house. He had inherited the vast property and business interests of his childless uncle Durgamohun Saha.

But he was affected by the modern times. He had been educated. He went to work with foreigners, wearing shoes and spoke proper English there. He had also grown a beard which meant that he had little chance of advancing in his career in the employ of the foreign trader. He was easily recognisable as a member of the new intelligentsia when one laid eyes on him.

In addition there was a reforming influence at home. His wife was beautiful. In combination with his college education, this meant total abandonment of the old ways. When they were unwell, they even went so far as to send for the assistant surgeon. Their food, clothes and style also took the same upward path.

Sir, you are most probably married and, therefore, it is completely unnecessary to tell you that ordinarily women love raw mangoes, hot chili peppers and strict husbands. The man unfortunate enough to be deprived of his wife's love is not ugly or poor; the truth is, he is too excessively mild.

If you ask why this happens, I have an answer as I have given much thought to it. One becomes unhappy unless able to exercise their instincts and abilities. A deer looks for a sturdy tree to rub its antlers against and finds no pleasure in doing that against the soft trunk of a banana plant. Ever since men and women have been separated by gender, women have been practicing the art of taming restless men by various means. The wife, whose husband is already tamed, finds herself in need of some other means of occupation; she finds all the weapons of tears, anger and love she has received from generations of women completely fruitless.

Women value the love that they must earn by using their feminine power to seduce a man. If a husband is too good-natured to give his wife that opportunity it indicates bad times ahead for both him and his wife.

The man that learns the new ways and ideas loses the natural freedom of the barbarian instincts given to him by his Maker and makes the bonds of matrimony rather loose and relaxed. Our unfortunate Phanibhushan had been spat out by the machinery of modernity as an extremely mild-natured person, who could not hope to find great success either in business or in marriage.

His wife Monimalika was given affection without really trying, costly saris without crying a few tears and jewellery without any pretence at being inconsolably offended. Her woman's heart and her love had both stopped trying anymore. She now only took and never gave back anything. Her inoffensive and somewhat stupid husband used to think one must always give in order to receive something in return. He had clearly got it completely wrong.

The result was that she had started seeing her husband as a machine that was there to supply her with saris and jewellery; a machine so efficient that there had never been a need to oil its wheels and gears.

Even though Phanibhushan was born in Phoolbere, his place of work was here where he had to spend most of his time. In the house in Phoolbere, he had no mother of his own, but elderly aunts in abundance. But he had not married a beautiful woman for the sake of the comfort of these elderly relatives. Hence he brought his wife to live where he was, with him. But the difference between other rights and rights to a wife is that just keeping her with oneself, separated from others may not essentially mean that she will be more available.

His wife rarely spoke to the women of the neighbourhood; nor did she indulge a couple of Brahmins on special days with some food or a travelling mendicant with generous alms—these were not the kind of practices she ever resorted to. She never wasted a thing and hoarded all but the affection she received from her husband. Strangely, this extended to the preservation of her astounding beauty which had remained untouched by time. People said that she was just as fresh-faced at twenty four as she had been when she was fourteen. Those who have ice where their hearts should be, who do not give any space for the pain and suffering of love to take root within their breast, must remain fresher for longer, preserving themselves both from outside and within.

The Creator made Monimalika fruitless in one respect, like a vine with excessive leaves and growth by making her childless. In other words, he did not give her the one thing that she could have understood better than all the jewels in her iron safe, the one thing that could have melted her heart of ice with all the gentle heat of a spring sunrise and allowed her household to fill with affection.

Monimalika was good at housework. She never employed too many people. If there was something that she could do herself, she could not bear to pay someone else to do it. She did not waste time thinking of others nor did she love anyone, all she did was work and save. This meant that she never suffered from illness or unhappiness and reigned over endless good health, imperturbable peace and ever-increasing wealth.

For most husbands, this is enough since this is hard to obtain. One does not remember the waist unless there is a pain in the region. To be made continually aware through the day of the presence of one's wife due to excessive displays of her love is like backache. Excessive devotion to a husband may be a source of pride for a wife but is rarely pleasing for him. At least, that is what I feel.

Good sir! How much love one receives from a wife and just how much she holds back, to measure this daily with a pair of scales is hardly a man's job; let her do her work and I will do mine; this is what the mathematics of daily life is all about. Our Maker has not given men the ability to tell what hides in the unspoken, how much want there is in fulfillment, the indications left veiled by the obvious or the vast worlds within an atom because there has never been any need for that. When there is even a minute's lessening in a man's love, women will sit down to analyse it. They endlessly analyse to find the intention hidden in words and the real words that hide in intentions. This is because women find their strength in the love of men; that is the capital they trade in. When they learn how to turn their sails to that wind, their life finds what they seek. This is why the scales that measure love have been placed within a woman's heart and not within men.

But lately, men have achieved what the Creator did not give them. Poets have defeated the natural order and have given this priceless device, this divining rod to everyone. One cannot blame the Creator, he did make men and women with enough differences, but civilisation has removed those; today women are becoming more like men while men are becoming more feminine, leading to the departure of peace and discipline from the domestic scene. These days, before marriage, both groom and bride need to consider whether they are marrying a masculine individual or a womanly one.

You look annoyed. I stay alone here, away from my wife and many deeply philosophical things about life come to mind—I cannot say them to my students and that is why I say these to you. Please, spare some thought on these subjects.

The important thing is that even though there was never a lack of seasoning in his food and never too much lime with his betel leaf, Phanibhushan still felt irritated by a tiny nagging doubt in his heart. His wife had no faults, there was nothing perceptibly wrong and yet he was not happy. He noticed a void within his wife and tried to pour diamonds and pearls into it but those went into the iron safe, leaving the heart as empty as before. His uncle Durgamohun had never understood the finer nuances of love, had never craved it nor had given it away so easily and yet he had been much-loved by his own wife. Do not doubt this for once that one cannot be modern when it comes to matters of business and one must be a man first in order to be a husband.

> By this time jackals had started howling very loudly in the nearby bushes. This caused the teacher to pause in his story for a while. It felt just as though the humorous animals were laughing at either the teacher's theories on matrimony or the modern Phanibhushan's weaknesses. When their cackling and baying had settled, the surroundings seemed even quieter and the school master stared into the darkness with his huge shining eyes as he started on his story anew.

A problem cropped up in the complex workings of Phanibhushan's business. As a non-business minded person, it is hard for me to understand or explain what exactly happened. The main thing was that it became hard for him to get credit in the markets. If he had a spare hundred and fifty thousand rupees for just five days, he would have managed to show that as a guarantee and his business would have regained the wind in its sails.

The money was proving hard to find. The fear that news of his borrowing from local money lenders would damage his credit even further made him look to unknown sources for loans. But with them, there was the matter of having enough to offer as collateral for the loan.

If he could pawn his wife's jewellery, there would be little need for receipts and delays and things could be done quickly and easily.

Phanibhushan went to his wife with his problems but not at once. He could not go to her as easily as a husband should have been able to go to his wife. Unfortunately, he loved his wife with the same sort of love as a hero feels for the heroine in a poem, the kind of love that demands cautious footsteps and carefully-worded sentences, the kind that resembles the tremendous attraction between the sun and the earth but maintains the same vast distances that separate them.

Even so, in the poems, the hero may still have to raise the topic of loans, pawning and IOUs with the heroine, but this leads to the tune faltering and the words failing, a certain hesitation accompanies these needful words and sorrow dogs his steps. The unfortunate Phanibhushan could not forcefully say, 'Listen here, a situation has come up and I need your jewellery.'

He did say it, but he said it very meekly. When Monimalika hardened her expression and did not bother replying with a yes or no, he was terribly disappointed but he could not hurt her back. This was because he lacked the natural barbarity of a male. Where he could have taken by force, he did not even express his genuine sadness. Where love was the only right, he was of the opinion that he would not allow force to enter, even if it meant ruination. If one had attempted to rebuke him over this, he would have presented a well-reasoned argument about how just as he could not force the market to lend him money when he was seen to be a risk, he would not force his wife to give him her jewellery when she did not want do that of her free will. Credit to him was the same as love; the only place for force was the battlefield. Did the Creator make men this generous, this powerful and this mighty so that they could dispatch arguments so well? Did he have the time to sit and observe the gentle nuances and subtleties of someone's nature or if it improved him in any way?

Phanibhushan went off to Kolkata to find the money he needed by some other means, thanks to the natural pride that prevented him from demanding his wife's help.

Generally in life, a wife knows her husband far better than the husband knows his wife, but if a husband is excessively sensitive, this is never completely appreciated by his wife. Phanibhushan's wife did not really understand him. Very progressive men do not fall within the scope of the ancient beliefs that form the untutored expertise of women. These men are unique and just as mysterious as women. The usual general quotas within which one may fit ordinary men, such as boorish, stupid or even unseeing—are the ones within which the modern man defies being classified..

For this reason, Monimalika called on her preferred counsel for advice. She had a very distant cousin who was from her village and who now worked for Phanibhushan. He was not the type to advance far by hard work but he managed to make a living and even supplement that by virtue of his relationship with her.

Monimalika told him everything and asked, 'What do you advise now?'

He shook his head very wisely, indicating this was not a good turn of events. The wise rarely see any turn of events as good. He said, 'The fellow will never be able to come up with the money, he will come after your jewellery eventually.'

From what Monimalika knew of people, this was not just inevitable, it was also very logical. She grew extremely worried for she had no child. She did have a husband but she did not feel his presence within her heart. When she thought that the only thing of value to her, the one thing that she had raised like a child over the years—not an abstract idea like love but real gold, meant to shine at chest, throat and hair—would disappear into the bottomless pit of a failing business, her very heart froze. She asked, 'What can I do?'

Madhusudan said, 'Let me take you and your jewellery back home, while I still can.' Clever Madhu had already decided on a plan which would see him get a part of that wealth, possibly even most of it.

Monimalika immediately agreed to this proposal.

One evening during that rainy season a boat came and moored at this very jetty. Monimalika boarded the boat very early the following dawn, in dense darkness broken only by the calls of sleepless frogs, wrapped in a thick shawl that covered her from head to toe. Madhusudan, who was sleeping in the boat woke up and asked, 'Give me the jewellery box.' Moni answered, 'Later, let us set off now.'

The boat set sail and moved fast before the wind.

Monimalika had worn all her jewellery, one precious piece at a time, all through the night, there was not an inch uncovered on her body. She had a fear of taking her jewellery box and losing it to thieves. But she knew that if she wore them all, she would have to be killed before a single jewel was lost.

Madhusudan was unable to understand where the jewellery was as she had no case with her. He did not think of the possibility that her thick shawl disguised what she valued as much as her own person. She might not have been able to understand her husband Phanibhushan, but she knew enough to be able to see into Madhusudan's heart with ease.

Madhusudan left a note with the estate's clerk saying that he was taking the lady of the house home. The man had been working since Phanibhushan's father was running the business and he was very annoyed. He wrote a letter to his employer, a letter which filled as it was with spelling errors and incorrect language, still managed to express his view that it was not correct to show too much leniency to one's wife.

Phanibhushan understood what had gone through Monimalika's mind. He felt the hurt even more acutely because he thought of how he had not touched her jewels and was engaged in finding the money despite every chance of losing everything, and she had still suspected him! He exclaimed, 'She fails to recognise me, even today!'

Instead of becoming angered at this mistreatment, he only felt deeply hurt. A man is the sceptre of divine justice within which the Creator has concealed his lightning, and if man cannot flare up in rage at the injustice wrought upon him and others, then shame upon him! Men are meant to be inflamed easily like forest fires while women will shed tears like rain at the slightest excuse. This was the Creator's design, but that does not apply anymore.

In his thoughts Phanibhushan said to his erring wife, 'If this is to be your decision, let it be, I will keep doing my duty.' The tragedy was that a man like Phanibhushan, who should have come along a few centuries later when conscience would be all that would be needed to rule the world, had been born in the nineteenth century and had married just the kind of primeval female whose wisdom was called catastrophic in the Scriptures. He did not write a single line to her and promised himself, he would never mention this to his wife ever again. What a strange punishment!

After managing somehow to obtain the money, a redeemed Phanibhushan came home ten days later. He felt certain that Monimalika would have returned after leaving the jewellery with her parents. As he approached the bedroom door he cast aside the air of supplication he had worn the previous time and thought of how Moni might be ashamed and slightly repentant to see him after his success.

He saw that the door was barred. He broke the padlock and found the room empty. In a corner lay the iron chest without a trace of any jewellery. Suddenly he felt a pang of remorse as he thought of how meaningless life was and how false were the ideas of love and success. We bleed on every spike of the cage that we build but there is no bird within and it does not stay even if we place it there. Then what have we been adorning with rubies wrought from blood and pearls garnered from tears! He kicked the empty dreams of family life far away.

He did not want to look for her. He thought to himself if she wanted to, she would come back. The old Brahmin rent collector came and said to him, 'What good can come of waiting and doing nothing, we have to look for her.' When he sent word to her parents' village, word came back that neither Moni nor Madhu had reached there.

This led to a wider search for both. People were sent to ask along the river banks. The police were informed so that Madhu could be located but no information could be unearthed about the boat or who the boatman had been or the route that they had taken.

One day, Phanibhushan entered his former bedroom in the evening after all hope had been abandoned. It was Janmashtami and it had been raining the whole day. There was a fair in the village to celebrate the holy day and a play had been organised in the community hall. The continual sound of heavy rain had lessened the sound of the voices singing in the play. Do you see that window where the shutter hangs loosely? That was where Phanibhushan was sitting alone in the darkness—with no heed to the cold wind, the splatter of rain and the songs entering the room. There was a pair of Art Studio paintings of Lakshmi and Saraswati on the wall while a couple of towels hung from the rack beside two carefully-folded saris, one with stripes and the other one with thin bands on the border, both ready to be used. Some dried up *paan*, made by Monimalika, lay in a brass bowl on a side table.

Inside the China cabinet were the porcelain dolls she had collected along with bottles of perfume, coloured glass decanters, fancy playing cards, large seashells and even empty soap boxes that she had saved with great care. The little round kerosene lamp that she would prepare each evening to be lit in the alcove still sat there, unlit and dimmed. That lamp was the sole wordless witness to her last minutes in the room; even the one who went away taking everything with her left behind so many things to remember her by, so much of her history, so many little touches of her once-living soul upon all these inanimate objects!

'Come Monimalika, light your lamp, illuminate your room, stand before your mirror and wear your carefully-folded sari, all your things await you. No one expects anything from you, just come back and allow your eternal youth and your undiminished beauty to lend life to these many scattered lifeless objects, to bind them together, for their unspoken cries have made this house a graveyard.'

Later on in the night, the rain and the singing must have stopped. Phanibhushan was still seated near the window. Such was the unbroken pitch darkness outside the window that he felt he was waiting before the sky-high gates of Hell, that if he cried out even things that had seemed lost forever might make an appearance. What if that lost gold flashed for once upon this jet black canvas of death, this infinitely hard immoveable barrier?

Suddenly a rattling sound accompanied by a tinkling of jewellery rose on the wind. It felt just as though the sound was coming from the jetty by the river. The river and the darkness of the night were indistinguishable from each other. Phanibhushan was thrilled and he kept searching the darkness with his eager eyes—both his heavy heart and eager eyes grew strained—and yet he could see nothing. The more his desire to see grew, the more darkness seemed to deepen and the world seemed to grow shadowy. Nature seemed to hastily draw curtains across the window of this house of death with greater care, sensing the arrival of a guest.

The sound gradually arrived on the topmost steps and started moving towards the house. It stopped at the main door, which the sentry had locked before going to see the play. A rattling and clanking sound rose as blows rained on the door. Phanibhushan could wait no longer. He went past the unlighted rooms, down the dark stairways and stood in front of the locked door. This was locked from the outside. As soon as he pushed it with all his strength, both the touch and the sound startled him and woke him up. He saw that he had walked downstairs in his sleep. He was drenched in sweat, his hands and feet were ice cold and his heart beat tremulously like a dying lamp. His dream broken, he found there were no sounds outside but the incessant sounds of rain and along with that the strains of the soiree from the village where the songs were now of the coming dawn.

Even though the entire incident was a dream, it felt so immediate and real that Phanibhushan thought very little now stood between him and the attainment of his impossible desire. The far away strains of Bhairavi and the sounds of rain seemed to say to him that he had woken into a real dream; that this world was actually the one with all the lies.

There was a play the following evening too and the doorman had been given a night off. Phanibhushan ordered the main door to be left open all night. The doorman said that it would not be wise to do that, seeing that there were many strangers in the village on occasion of the festival. Phanibhushan refused to listen to him. The man then declared that he would stay back and guard the house the whole night. Phanibhushan surprised him by announcing that there was no need for that and he would have to go to the soiree.

The next evening, Phanibhushan came and sat at the bedroom window after blowing the lamps out. The sky was filled with clouds that were pregnant with rain and there was a vague silence all around that seemed to be waiting for the evening to unfold. The croaking of the frogs and the sounds from the play could not penetrate that stillness but merely added a discordant note to it.

Very late at night, the frogs and the insects of the night and the distant songs from the village fell silent and a new darkness seemed to descend upon the night. It was apparent that the time was approaching.

Like the previous night, a clattering sound rose along with the tinkle of ornaments. But Phanibhushan did not heed that. He was afraid that his intense desire and restless attempts might thwart all his wishes and overwhelm his senses. He exerted every effort to control his mind and sat as still as a statue fashioned from wood.

The sounds were heard entering the house today after slowly moving from the jetty. They were heard ascending the circular stairway of the inner house. Phanibhushan could not control himself any more, his heart beat like a boat tossed about in a storm and he felt as though he would cease breathing. The sounds came closer along the verandah. All that was left was for it to cross the threshold.

He could not wait any longer. The emotions that he had bottled within him burst forth and he suddenly rose from the bed, calling out aloud, 'Moni!' He immediately woke and found that the very panes of the windows of the room shook with the fervour in his call. The orchestra of frog song and the tired voices of the singers in the village play could be heard outside. Phanibhushan clapped his hand to his brow.

The next day, the village fair ended. The merchants and the travelling company of singers went away. Phanibhushan ordered that everyone would have to go away and leave him alone that evening, once darkness had fallen. The servants surmised that he was engaging in the occult. Phanibhushan did not touch any food for the whole of that day.

He came and sat by the window of that empty house. There were patches of clear sky that night and the stars looked brilliant as they glittered through the clear rain swept breeze. There was still a long while to go before the moon appeared in the sky. The end of the fair meant a complete absence of boats on the river while the villagers were all immersed in a deep sleep after two nights of revelry.

Phanibhushan sat on a bed and leaned against the headrest watching the stars; he was thinking about a time when he was nineteen and at college in Kolkata, lying on the grass near Goldighi and looking up at those eternal stars. He remembered Moni in her riverside room, fourteen years old, the subtle changes of womanhood already upon her, her bright young face, the sweet pain they had felt in that separation and how the stars had seemed to pulse to the rhythm of his youthful longing, to the tune of Basanta Raga. Those same stars today seemed to shine with fire across the sky tonight and say 'How varied is life!'

One by one all the stars in the sky were extinguished. A sheet of darkness descended from the heavens and seemed to join the darkness that covered the earth like a pair of eyelids folding in unison. Phanibhushan was calm tonight. He was certain that his wish would be fulfilled today; that death would reveal its secrets to his questions.

The sound rose from the river currents, up the stone steps as it had done the night before. Phanibhushan closed his eyes and sat in meditation, his heart steeled against what might happen. The rattling came past the sentry-less entrance and continued to rise up the spiral staircase; it came down the long verandah and finally paused for a while at the door to the bedroom.

Phanibhushan's heart grew anxious and his whole body thrilled with fear but he did not open his eyes tonight. The sound crossed the threshold and entered the dark room. It went and stood at each of the places where the saris lay folded, the kerosene lamp stood unlit in its corner, the dried *paan* sat in a container on a table and the cabinet filled with various ornaments waited for appreciation. Finally it came to a halt before him.

Phanibhushan opened his eyes and saw that the newly risen moonlight had filled the room and there was a skeleton standing by his bed. It wore rings on all its fingers, gold wristlets upon its palms, bangles and armlets on its arms, necklaces and headpieces, every bone was glittering with diamonds and gold. The ornaments dangled loosely but still managed to stay on the apparition. The most terrifying aspect of this being was the presence of life in its eyes in the midst of the skull, its irises dark and shaded by long lashes, lively and steadfast as they looked at him. Eighteen years ago, the same pair of beautiful dark eyes that he had first looked into during his marriage as the celebratory flutes played happy tunes around them were now staring back at him by the pale moonlight of a rainy night. His blood froze and he tried desperately to close his eyes against the sight but he could not; his eyes remained open in a lifeless stare.

The skeleton then looked at Phanibhushan's astounded face intently and raised its left hand in silent beckoning. Diamond rings flashed on the bones of its fingers.

Phanibhushan stood up uncomprehendingly. The skeleton walked to the door, a clanking from the jewellery rattling against its bones rising about it. He followed it like a puppet. Past the verandah, down the spiral stairs in the dense darkness went the dry clattering of bones and the tinkling of jewellery. They crossed the verandah downstairs and entered the unlighted foyer; from there they finally reached the gravelled garden path. The stones crunched under bony footfall. The pale moonlight could not escape from that garden surrounded by thick foliage; they walked together through the rain-perfumed darkness of that shadowed path lit by the glow of firefly swarms till they arrived at the banks of the river.

The skeleton continued to descend, thumping on at an unwavering speed, one pace at a time down the same steps it had climbed up so recently. A long moonlit streak gleamed on the fast flow of the rain swollen river.

The skeleton descended into the river and Phanibhushan followed it. As soon as his feet touched the water his trance broke. His guide was no longer there, the trees on the banks were standing still and a segment of the moon was shining above their tops, calm and wondering. Phanibhushan faltered repeatedly on uncertain footsteps and fell into the current. Even though he did know how to swim, he had no control over his nerves and after hovering on the brink of wakefulness for a few seconds after being in a dream he immediately fell back into a sleep from which there could be no return.'

Once the story was finished, the teacher stopped for a while. It was immediately clear that everything else had fallen silent apart from him. I was quiet for a long time and he could not see my expression as we sat in the dark.

'Do you not believe in this?' he asked me.

I asked, 'Do you believe in this?'

He said, 'No, I will tell you why I do not. Firstly, Mother Nature does not write novels, she has much else to do.'

'Secondly, Phanibhushan Saha is actually my name.'

The school teacher said without a trace of shame, 'I guessed correctly then. What was your wife's name?'

I answered, 'Nrityakali.'

(Monihara – Golpo Guchcho)

The Final Night

'Aunt?'

'Go to sleep Jatin, it is late.'

'Let it be late, I do not have much time left. I was saying perhaps Moni could be sent to her parents, I forget where her father lives ....'

'In Sitarampur.'

'Yes to Sitarampur; send Moni to them. How much longer will she have to look after an invalid? She is not that strong herself.'

'Listen to yourself! Why would your wife want to go away while you lie ill here?'

'Does she know what the doctor said?'

'Even if she does not know what he said, she has eyes that can see. The other day, as soon as I hinted at going to her parents' house, she burst into tears.'

It is important to clarify that was some distortion of the truth in what the aunt had said. Her conversation with Moni had been along the following lines:

'Daughter, is there some news from your parents' house? I thought I saw your cousin Anath.'

'Yes, my mother has sent word that my sister's rice ceremony will be held next Friday. I was thinking ...'

'Well child, why not send a gold necklace, your mother will be pleased.'

'I am thinking of going. I have not seen this young sister yet, I wish to see her so very much.'

'But how you will go, leaving Jatin in this state? Surely you have heard what the doctor said?'

'But the doctor said, there is still no sign ...'

'Be as it may, how will you go away when he is so unwell?'

'This is the only sister I have, after three brothers, she is much loved—and I have heard the ceremony will be held with a lot of pomp—if I am not there, my mother will be very...'

'I do not pretend to understand what your mother will think, my child. But if you go home while Jatin is in this state, I can tell you that your father will be angry.'

'I know. But if you write one line to him saying that there is nothing to worry about—it will be alright if I leave him ...'

'You do not have to tell me that there will be little difference to how Jatin is cared for even if you go. But if I do have to write to your father, I will disclose all that is on my mind.'

'Fine, you do not have to do it. If I go and speak to my husband he will agree...'

'Look daughter, I have put up with a lot—but if you go to Jatin with this request, I will not bear it at all. Your father knows you too well; you will not be able to fool him.'

The aunt left after saying this. Moni lay on her bed and fumed at the injustice.

Her friend from next door came to see her and asked, 'What is this, why the glum face?'

'Look at what is happening, it is the rice ceremony for my only sister and these people are not letting me go!'

'Dear God, what are you saying? How will you go? Your husband is so ill.'

'I do not have to do anything for him, I couldn't, even if I tried. Everyone is so quiet, I feel stifled. I am just saying that I cannot live like this.'

'You are truly amazing!'

'Look my friend, I am not as good at pretences as you might be. But it is not in my nature to sit quietly in a corner, for fear of people saying things.'

'So, what is it that you will do, pray tell me.'

'I will go and no one can stop me from doing that.'

'You know, you have some gall! I am going, I have got better things to do.'

When Jatin heard that Moni had shed tears over being prevented from visiting her parents' home, he was quite moved. As he sat up and propped himself against a pillow, he said, 'Aunt, can you open this window a little wider? I don't think this light is needed any more.'

As soon as the window was opened the silent night appeared at the invalid's door like a traveller walking the eternal path to salvation. Stars that had borne witness to innumerable deaths since time immemorial, looked down from above at Jatin.

He could see his beloved Moni's face shimmering upon that vast darkened firmament. Her eyes were brimming with tears—incessant, unspilled for all time.

His aunt was reassured to see him silent for so long and hoped that he might have fallen asleep at last.

But he suddenly spoke up, 'Aunt, you and others have always said that Moni is a restless girl who has never been able to feel settled in this house. But see how …'

'No, my child, I misunderstood her—I know better now that I have had time.'

'Aunt!'

'Jatin, sleep my dear.'

'Let me think of things, let me speak. Do not be annoyed with me.'

'No, of course not, please speak.'

'I was thinking, it takes people so much time even to understand themselves. Once upon a time when I thought that she would not be able to love us, I used to bear it in silence. At that time you all …'

'Do not say that! I put up with a lot too.'

'But the mind is not a lump of clay that one can just pick up and make one's own. I knew that she had not found the key to her own heart; that a great blow would surely fall one day and …'

'You are right.'

'That is why I never minded all her childishness.'

The aunt said nothing to this but a sigh escaped her lips.

She had noticed how Jatin had often spent entire nights outside on the verandah, despite getting drenched by the windswept rain. How many times had he lain in his bed, clutching his head in agony, hoping that Moni would come and press his temples but the girl had been preoccupied with getting dressed to go to the theatre with her friends. She would come to fan him to sleep and he would push her away; she knew how much pain was hidden in that anger. She had so often wanted to tell Jatin, 'My child, do not pay so much attention to that girl. Allow her to truly want something—for into each life must come some tears.' But these are not things that one can say easily, nor do people understand. He had created a shrine for all womanhood in his heart and Moni was the deity he had placed within. He could not imagine that he would have to wait forever for her largesse and so he worshipped her and kept hoping for her love.

Just as she thought that he might have gone back to sleep, he said, 'I know, you once thought that I have not found happiness with Moni. That angered you but truly happiness is like those distant stars; it does not shut out all darkness, it leaves cracks in between. How many mistakes have I made in life, how many things have I misunderstood but there have still been glimmers of bliss shining through. Why else would my heart have received the joy that I feel today!'

His aunt stroked his brow gently. No one saw the tears she shed in the darkness.

'I am thinking of how she will survive, given how young she is.'

'Jatin, surely she is not that young? This is the right age. I too had to turn to God at a young age—what harm has it done me? What is this need for happiness any way!'

'But Aunt, just as Moni's mind begins to bloom, I…'

'Why think about all that Jatin? If her mind does bloom, that is good fortune I suppose.'

Suddenly Jatin remembered a song he had heard a travelling mendicant sing a long time ago:

Oh mind, while you slept unaware
Your beloved came to the door.
The sounds of departure woke you
But it was in darkness.

'What is the time, Aunt?'

'Probably nine o'clock.'

'Only nine o'clock? I thought it would have been at least three o' clock. My midnight starts as soon as the sun sets. Then why were you so eager for me to go to sleep?'

'Last night you talked for so long that you could not sleep till very late That was why I thought of telling you to go to sleep earlier today.'

'Is Moni asleep?'

'No, she is making lentil soup for you before she goes to sleep.'

'Really Aunt, does she really do that…..'

'She is the one cooking the invalid diet for you each day. Do you think she gets any rest?'

'But I used to think that she…..'

'Do women really need to be taught any of this? They do it when the need arises.'

'The fish stew I had for lunch was so well prepared. I thought you had made it.'

'What are you saying! Does she let me do anything? She washes your towels herself and dries them. She knows that you cannot bear any dirt anywhere. If you could see your front room, you would see how she keeps it spick and span twice a day. If I let her be here, she would end up being here all the time. That is just what she wants to do.'

'Is she not well'

'The doctors say she can do it all. It is just that she is so soft hearted that she would fall ill in a very short time if she saw you in pain.'

'Aunt, how do you stop her from coming here?'

'I can do it only because she is so fond of me. I still have to go and give her frequent health reports—one of the many things I have to do.'

The stars flickered like eyes filled with tears of compassion. Jatin paid his respects to the life that was about to leave him today—and placed himself in the hands of Death with a sort of patient belief.

Jatin let out a sigh, fidgeted a little and asked his Aunt, 'If she is awake, could you call her once?'

'I will get her right away, my child.'

'I will not detain her here for too long—only five minutes or so—I just need to say a few words to her….'

The Aunt sighed heavily and went to fetch Moni. Jatin's pulse quickened. He knew that he had not been able to have a proper conversation with Moni in all their days together. It is hard for two discordant instruments to play together.

It was quite common for Jatin to feel jealous of Moni when he heard the sounds of frivolous merry-making from her and her friends. He blamed himself of course—why had he never learned to have light heart edconversations like that. It is not as if he couldn't. After all, he did it all the time with his friends. But a man's light hearted banter is very different from that of a woman. It is easy to have a monologue on a serious topic but light topics demand attention from others. A flute can play alone but a cymbal must have a partner to create a din. That was why Jatin had sat down with Moni quite often in the evenings and after a few desultory words, the conversation had dried up so completely that the silence in the air seemed to oppress the very evening. Jatin understood that Moni badly wanted to escape and ardently wished that a third person might appear; it is hard to have a conversation between two people but not between three.

Jatin thought of what he would say when Moni eventually came to him. If he thought too long the words became too serious. He worried that he would waste the five minutes that he had asked for. And yet he knew that he did not have too many of these moments of peace left in his life.

'What is this? Are you going somewhere?'

'I am going to Sitarampore.'

'What! Who are you going with?'

'Anath is taking me.'

'Darling child, go if you must, I will not come in your way. Just not today.'

'I have reserved a ticket.'

'Let that be. That will be a loss you will have to bear—go tomorrow as early as you can. Just do not go today.'

'Aunt, I do not follow your rules about the right days to travel. What harm is there in going today?'

'Jatin has called you. He wants to say something to you.'

'There is still a little time left, I can go and talk to him now.'

'No, you cannot tell him that you are going away.'

'Alright, I will not say anything. But I cannot be late as the ceremony at my parents' home is tomorrow. I must go today.'

'I am entreating you daughter. Just listen to me once for today. Go and sit with him today. Do not rush things.'

'But what can I do, the train will not wait for me. Anath has already gone. He will be back in ten minutes to take me. I will quickly go and see what he wants.'

'No, let it be. Go then. I do not want you to visit him like this. You wretch! The one you cause such pain will leave everything behind and disappear tomorrow—but you will be haunted by this day forever. As surely as there is a god, you will learn this some day.'

'Aunt, do not curse me like this.'

'My dear son! Why are you still alive! Is there no end to this evil—how can I hold this back from you!'

The aunt went back to the invalid after a while. She hoped that Jatin would fall asleep. But she saw him move as soon as she entered the room. She spoke to him saying, 'She has really done it this time!'

'What has happened? Did Moni not come? Why are you so late Aunt?'

'I went and found that she was weeping because she had burnt some milk she was heating for you. I tried to console her and told her that there was no harm done as there was more milk in the house. But she is so ashamed that she burnt your milk because of her own carelessness. I consoled her with great difficulty and made her lie down. I don't think she should come here tonight, let her sleep.'

Jatin felt sad that Moni did not visit him but also relieved that she was not there. He had been apprehensive that her physical presence would overshadow the glorious image that he had conjured in his mind. He was after all used to this. His heart took pride in the knowledge that she had felt ashamed after burning the milk meant for him.

'Aunt!'

'What is it, son?'

'You know quite well that my life is almost over. But I have no regrets. You must not mourn me.'

'No my darling, I will not mourn you. I do not believe that life is all redemption and there is none in death.'

'Aunt, I tell you, I think death seems sweet to me.'

Jatin looked at the sky where it seemed his beloved Moni had come to him decked as death. She was a woman in the full bloom of her health, surrounded by family, children and compassion.

Those stars were the celestial blessings garlanded through her hair. He felt that the night was like a veil that was spread over their heads to unite them once again. The vast darkness grew luminous with the love in her eyes. The mistress of this house, his little Moni took on the form of the world, as she ascended the stars to take her throne where life mingled with death. The night flowed with sanctity. Jatin thought, 'At last, you come to me, shedding your façade in this darkness—how much sorrow have you caused me! Beautiful one, you will not escape me any more.'

'Aunt, I am hurting but not as much as you think. It is as if I am removing myself from my pain. It was like a full boat that was tied to the ship that is my life all these days; but today the ties have been undone, and it has begun to drift away. I still see it, but it does not feel like it is related to me any more. Aunt, I have not seen Moni in the last two days.'

'Will I place another pillow behind you?'

'I feel that Moni too has left, like that boat carrying all my sadness.'

'Dear, drink a little pomegranate juice. Your throat must be getting dry.'

'I wrote my will yesterday—did I show that to you? I cannot recall.'

'I have no need to see it, Jatin'

'When my mother died, I had nothing. You are the one that took me in, that is why I was saying…'

'What kind of talk is that! I only had this house and a little property. Everything else is what you have achieved.'

'But this house…'

'Where is that little house? You have added so much to it. It is hardly there any more.'

'Moni might not show it but she does…'

'Do you think I do not know that Jatin? Now, sleep a little.'

'I have left her everything but it will all be yours. She will never disobey you.'

'Why are you worrying about that, my child!'

'Everything I have is through your blessing. I do not want that you should see my will and ever feel that …'

'What a thing to say! Why would I mind if you give what is already yours to Moni? Am I that wretched? My happiness is only increased by the joy you feel in being able to give what is yours to her.'

'But I have also…'

'Look here Jatin. Now I will have to get angry with you. You will slip away and you want me to wallow in the money you leave me.'

'Aunt, if only I could give you something more than money…'

'You have Jatin, you have. You filled my empty heart when I needed it the most. I will not complain today if my rights have ceased. Give it all away—the house, all the property, all the holdings—write it all away to her! I would not be able to bear the weight.'

'You will not need anything but Moni is still young and that is why…'

'Do not say that, please. Give her all if you must but do not talk of age as an excuse for… '

'Why shouldn't she enjoy herself, Aunt?'

'No, she will not. I am saying she will not be able to enjoy anything. Her throat will dry up!'

Jatin fell silent. He could not tell whether the prospect of Moni languishing in his absence was true or false or whether it filled him with sadness or joy. The stars seemed to come and whisper into his ears, 'This is all a farce. We have seen it all for a thousand years and more.'

Jatin said with a sigh, 'We cannot leave behind the things that really matter.'

'You are not leaving her bereft. Will she not appreciate the generosity of your gifts to her at all? I bless her so that she may know one day what you have left her with.'

'Give me some more pomegranate juice, my mouth feels so dry. Did Moni visit me yesterday? I cannot remember.'

'She did. You were asleep. She sat at your head for a long time and fanned you. Then she went to give your clothes to the washerman.'

'Astonishing! I must have been dreaming at that very same time that she was trying to come to me, that she was pushing the door open but it would not let her enter. But I think this is wrong of you to let her see that I am dying. I fear she may be very affected later when I do go.'

'Child, let me pull the shawl over your legs, the soles of your feet are cold to the touch.'

'No, I don't want any covers.'

'Do you know Jatin that this shawl was made by Moni? She has been working late at night to finish this for you. She finished making it only last night.'

Jatin took the shawl in his hands and examined it a little. It felt as if the wool bore the softness of Moni's feelings and that she had woven the love she felt into the fibres of the shawl, as she worked through the nights. He felt not just the wool but also the softness of her fingers in the weave. When his aunt placed the shawl across his legs, he felt it was Moni herself touching his feet to comfort him through the nights of wakefulness.

'But Aunt, I thought Moni could not knit, that she did not like doing these things at all.'

'How long does it take if one truly sets her mind to it? I had to show her how to do it—there are many mistakes as well in the work.'

'Let them be. This is not going to an exhibition in Paris. This will do fine for me.'

He felt happy knowing that there were many mistakes in the work. She could not do it well, she did know how to but she still sat night after night to finish this for him—this imbued the event with a kind of tragic pathos in his eyes. He took up the shawl in his hands again.

'Aunt, is the doctor downstairs?'

'Yes, he will stay here tonight.'

'But do not give me any sleeping medicines. You have seen how they do not put me to sleep but only make me feel worse. Let me stay awake tonight. Aunt, tomorrow is the twelfth night of this lunar cycle—we were married on this night. Tomorrow the stars in the sky will be the same ones that burned that night. Perhaps Moni does not remember—I want to remind her tonight. Just call her here for a few minutes. Why are you quiet? Perhaps the doctors have told you I am weak, that I do not need the excitement. But I am telling you, if I can speak to her tonight I will feel great peace and not even need sleeping pills. That is why I have not slept for the past two nights; because I have something I need to tell her. Aunt, do not cry like that. I am fine. My heart feels fuller than it has for a long time. That is why I want her. I feel that I would be able to give my fulfilled heart to her today. There were many things that I have wanted to say to her, but I could not. But I cannot delay this any more. Call her now for there will be no time later. No, Aunt, I cannot bear these tears of yours. You have borne everything so far, why break down now?'

'Jatin, I thought all my tears were done and finished—but now I see that there are more to be shed. I cannot bear it any more.'

'Call for Moni—I will tell her about tomorrow night…'

'I am going. Shambhu is waiting outside the door. Tell him if you need anything.'

His aunt went to Moni's bedroom and sat on the floor there. She called, 'Come, just once! Come, you wretch, and answer the prayers of the man who has given you his all—he is dying now, do not hasten that any more.'

Jatin started at the sound of footsteps and asked, 'Moni?'

'No, it is I, Shambhu. Did you call for me?'

'Could you ask your mistress to come here once.'

'Who?'

'My wife.'

'But she has not come back yet.'

'Where has she gone?'

'To Sitarampore.'

'Did she leave today?'

'No, she has been there for three days.'

Jatin felt his skin tremble and darkness cloud his eyes for a while. He slumped back on the bed. He pushed the shawl away with his feet.

When his aunt returned after a long while, he did not speak of Moni. She thought that he had forgotten the reason for her absence.

He suddenly asked her, 'Did I tell you about the dream I had the other day?'

'Which dream?'

'The one where Moni was pushing the door open but the door would not be opened. She looked at me from outside but she never came in. She has done that all her life. I have called her to me so often but she never really wanted to belong.'

His aunt said nothing in answer. She thought, 'The little illusion that I had made for him with my lies is gone as well. It is best that he accepts his sorrow—there is no point in trying to disguise this with trickery.'

'Dear Aunt, the love I received from you will be the treasure I will take from this life of mine. In another life you will surely be born as my daughter and I will take care of you as you deserve.'

'What are you saying Jatin? Another birth as a woman? Why can I not be a son to you? Pray for that instead!'

'No, not a son. You will come to me as beautiful as you were in your youth. I have a notion of how I want to dress you.'

'Enough Jatin! Now sleep a little.'

'I will give you the name Lakshmirani.'

'But surely, that is not a modern name?'

'No it is not. But Aunt, you are of a time long gone. I want you to bring that with you when you come to me again.'

'I do not want to bring the burden of a daughter to your life.'

'Do you think me to be weak? Do you wish to save me from sadness?'

'Child, I have a woman's heart and I am the one who is weak—that is why I have always tried to protect you from every hurt all my life. But what have I done for you? Nothing!'

'Aunt, I have not managed to apply what I have learned in life. But these lessons will not be in vain. I will show what I can do in the next life. I now know that it is a waste of time to keep looking inward all throughout life.'

'But whatever you say, you have received nothing! You have only given!'

'Aunt, I am proud of one thing. I have never insisted on happiness. Never have I said, this is my right and I will have it. I take only what is given willingly. I wanted the thing that does not come with a guarantee and waited all my life to have it. If I had not wanted falsehood, I would not have had to wait for such a long time—perhaps now, truth will prevail. Who is there? Who is that?'

'There is no one there, Jatin…'

'Will you go and check the other room, I am sure…'

'No my child, I did not see anyone.'

'But I clearly heard…'

'No Jatin, the doctor is here.'

The Doctor said, 'Look, he talks too much if you are here with him. This is what has kept him awake for the last couple of nights. Go and sleep, the nurse will watch him tonight.'

'No Aunt, you may not go.'

'Let me go and sit there my child.'

'No, you will stay by my side—I am not letting go of your hand, not till the very end. I was raised by these two hands and God must come and take me from their embrace.'

'All right, but you must not talk so much, Sir. It is time for that other medicine…'

'Is it time? All lies! The time is long gone. Now is the turn to console with medicines and words. I do not need any of that. I am not afraid of dying. Why try and send Death away? Why have you gathered all these doctors? Send them away, all of them. I only want you and no one else, none of these lies!'
'This agitation is not good for you!'

'Is it time? No, I do not believe that. The time is past.'

'Then you should go, do not agitate me. Has the doctor left? Can you come and sit here on the bed so that I can sleep with my head on your lap?'

'Alright, sleep a little, my dear.'

'No, Aunt, do not ask me to sleep—what if I should never awaken! I still need to be awake for a little longer. Can you not hear? She is coming! She will be here soon.'

'Dear Jatin, open your eyes once and see who is here—just once please.'

'Who is it? Is it a dream?'

'Not a dream, it is Moni and your father-in-law.'

'Who are you?'

'Can you not recognise her, she is your Moni!'

'Moni, is that door open?'

'They are all open, my child!'

'No Aunt, that is not a shawl across my legs, that is not what I want, that was all lies!'

'It is not a shawl Jatin. It is your wife, falling on your feet—bless her a little! Do not cry so much my child, the time to mourn will soon be upon us—but for now, calm yourself.'

(Shesher Ratri – Golpo Guchcho)

At Night

'Doctor! Doctor!'

'How annoying to be woken so late at night,' I thought to myself as I opened my eyes to realise it was my landlord Dakshinacharan Babu. I quickly got up and dragged the backless chair for him to sit and looked at his eyes anxiously. The clock had struck 2.30.

Dakshinacharan looked pale as he stared at me and said, 'That problem started again tonight— your medicines did not help.'

I said with some trepidation, 'Perhaps you have increased your drinking again.'

He grew very annoyed and said, 'That is very wrong of you. It is not alcohol; but you will never guess what it is unless I tell you.'

I turned up the little lamp that was burning dimly in the alcove and it gave off a little light and a lot of smoke. I covered my feet and sat on a packing box with a newspaper spread on top of it. He began to tell me his story.

It would be hard to find a woman who was as good a homemaker as my first wife. But I was still young and full of romantic notions. In addition to that, I had a habit of reading poetry and thus I was not greatly impressed by efficient housekeeping. I often thought of a couplet by the poet Kalidasa:

Grihini sachiboh sakhi mitoh
Priyashishya lalite kalabidhou
A wife must be both secretary and confidante
As well as favoured student in the arts of pleasure.

But my wife was unmoved by the instructions of the *Lalita Kabya* and she would dismiss any attempts to address her as a beloved friend, with laughter. Poetic verses and affectionate names dissolved away in the face of her smiles, just as Indra's elephant Airavat was swept away by the currents of the river Ganga. She had an amazing ability for laughter.

About four years ago, I became gravely ill. I became delirious with fever after an infection and it was even thought that I might die. The doctors came and said we were to prepare for the worst. But one of my relatives brought a holy man to see me and the fellow gave me a mixture of a root pounded in ghee. I am not sure whether it was that or simple luck but I recovered from the illness.

During the entire time that I was ill, my wife did not rest for a moment, whether during the day or at night. Even though she was but one woman, she fought off the messengers of death that gathered about our door and protected an undeserving wretch such as me like a helpless child, with all the love and compassion of her heart. She paid little heed to her need for food, sleep or her surroundings.

But while death withdrew its hold on me in defeat, it managed to leave a mark on my wife.

She had been with a child at the time but she gave birth to a dead infant shortly afterwards. After that she fell ill with various serious illnesses. I began to nurse her, much to her embarrassment. She would say, 'What are you doing? What will people say if they see you fussing over me? Please do not come into my room at all hours of the day and night like that!'

If I fanned her while pretending to fan myself at night while she was feverish, she would try to snatch the fan from me as soon as she knew what I was doing. If my meals were ever delayed by ten minutes because I had been tending to her, she would make me swear a hundred times that it would never happen again. Any little act of nursing led to an upheaval. She would say, 'It is not right that men should be so agitated.'

I think you have seen our house in Baranagore. There is a garden in front of the house and the river flows right next to the garden. There is a part of the garden immediately to the south of our bedroom where she created a walled garden of her own, that she enclosed with a hedge of henna shrubs. That was the least ornate part of the entire garden, with only plants commonly found in the region. That is to say, in that part of the garden, colour did not compete with perfume, leaves did not shame flowers into hiding their faces and no one had festooned stakes with labels which were inscribed with plant names in Latin, in pots planted with inconspicuous plants. It was planted mainly with jasmine, roses, gardenias, oleanders and tuberoses. The base of an enormous mimosa tree was surrounded by white marble. She used to have it washed clean twice a day when she had been well. That was her place to come and sit down when she had a break from her duties in summer. One could see the river from the position but the Company's men on the river boats could not see her.

After being confined to her bed for many days, one moonlit night she said, 'I feel so strange locked away in this room; let us go and sit in that garden of mine.'

I helped her to walk to the stone seat beneath the mimosa tree with great care and laid her upon it. I could have cradled her head upon my knee but that would have seemed odd to her and so I brought a pillow that I placed beneath her head.

The light of the full moon fell on her wasted face filigreed by the shade of the branches overhead and the tree gently shed a few flowers upon us. As I looked at her face beside me in that densely perfumed shadowed silence, I felt tears welling in my eyes.

I slowly moved closer to the tree, took one of her frail hands in mine and felt her feverish skin. She did not say anything to me. I felt quite emotional after sitting in silence for a while and said, 'I will never forget the love you have given me.'

I immediately knew that there was no need to say such a thing. My wife laughed out at this. There was a little shyness, happiness and some disbelief in her laugh as well as a lot of mirth at my expense. She did not say a word in protest but her smile said it all; 'It is not possible to be remembered eternally and I do not even wish for that to happen.'

That sweet knowing laugh was exactly why I had always feared to talk of love with my wife. The things I thought of saying to her while away from her, seemed frivolous when I found myself in her presence. I still do not understand why words that would bring tears to the eyes if read should have caused so much laughter whenever I tried to say them.

One can respond to words but there is no arguing with laughter and thus I had to be silent. The moonlight grew brighter and a faraway cuckoo would call incessantly. I sat and thought whether his mate too was silent on such a beautiful night.

None of her symptoms showed any signs of lessening with every kind of medical treatment. The doctor said, 'Perhaps a change of scene might do her some good.' So I took her to Allahabad.

> Here Dakshinacharan suddenly stopped his story. He gave me a suspicious look and then cradled his head in his arms and thought for a while. I waited in silence. The kerosene lamp flickered in its alcove and the buzzing of mosquitoes in the room became quite obvious. Just as abruptly, he began speaking again.

There my wife was being treated by Haraan Daktar. After many days had passed with no change to her condition, the doctor spoke to us about something both me and my wife had already begun to understand; she was not going to get any better and would always be an invalid. Soon afterwards she said to me, 'When I am not going to get better and there is little hope of my death any time soon, how long do you intend to spend with this half dead creature? I feel that you should re-marry.'

She said it as if it was the reasonable thing to do. There was no indication of the fact that she was being very brave and noble by saying this.

Now it was my turn to laugh. But was I able to? I spoke instead like a literary hero and said evenly, 'As long as I am alive…'

She interrupted and said, 'Yes, yes! You need not say any more. I find your words so funny.'

I would not be turned from my path and continued, 'I will not be able to love anyone in this lifetime.'

She laughed at hearing this and I had to change the subject.

I do not know if I had clearly admitted this to myself, but I now understand that I had grown mentally exhausted with this futile nursing. I did not imagine not having to do it; but the thought of having to spend my entire life with this permanently unwell woman was painful to me. Alas, when I had faced life in the first flush of youth, it had seemed bright with hopes of affection, promises of happiness and illusions of love. On this day when I cast my eyes to the years ahead it seemed like a long, thirsty trudge through a desert paved with disappointment.

She must have seen the weariness that pervaded my care for her. I did not know it then but I have no doubt now that she read me as easily as a children's primer. That was why when I went to her as a lover from the pages of literature with many words to say, she laughed at me with so much affection and the inevitable humour. Today when I think that, like my Creator, she too knew all that which lay in the unknown parts of my heart, I feel like dying of shame and remorse.

The doctor was of the same caste as us. I was often invited to eat at his place. He introduced me to his daughter after I had known him for a short while. She was unmarried and about fifteen years old. Her father said he was yet to find someone suitable but I heard from others that the family had some other problems.

But she had not faults of her own. She was beautiful and well educated. Some nights, I would forget that I was supposed to be elsewhere as I chatted with her and I would come home very late, long past the time to give my wife her medicines. She knew I had gone to Haraan Doctor's house but she never once asked me what the reason for my delays was.

I began to see an oasis of hope in the desert that was my life, once again. A lake filled with clear water shimmered before me as I wrestled with my overpowering thirst. I could not rein my heart in and turn away from it.

The patient's room became even more joyless as a destination for me. I frequently forgot to go to her, and her medicines were often administered late or not at all.

The doctor often said to me that it was best for people without any hope of improvement in their condition to pass away; as they had little happiness in life and others were also inconvenienced. The view was not one that was out of the ordinary but he should not have expressed it in consideration for my wife's condition. But a doctor's mind is so blasé about life and death that I suppose, they do not appreciate how the rest of us feel.

One day I suddenly overheard my wife say to the doctor in the adjoining room, 'Why are you increasing the debt to the pharmacy with these useless medicines. When my life is itself the disease, why not give me a medicine that removes this life soon?'

The doctor answered her, 'Please do not say such things.'

I felt very hurt when I heard the words. I went to her room when the doctor had gone, sat by her bed and stroked her forehead gently. She said to me, 'This room is very warm, go somewhere else. It is time for your walk anyway. If you don't take a walk, you never feel hungry at dinner.'

Going for a walk meant going to the doctor's house. I was the one who had convinced her that it was necessary to take a walk in order to feel hungry. I am certain now that she saw through my artifice. I was stupid and thought that I had fooled her.

After saying this, Dakshinacharan remained silent for a long time, his face hidden in his hands. He finally said, 'Give me a glass of water.' He then continued with his story.

One day the doctor's daughter Manorama expressed a wish to come and see my wife. I do not know why, but I did not like this idea at all. But I had no valid reason to refuse her. She came to the house one evening.

That day my wife was in more pain than usual. She had the habit of being stiller and more silent on such days; the only outward signs would be an occasional clenching of her fists and a blue tinge that appeared over her face. There wasn't a sound in the room and I was sitting by the edge of her bed. She was unable to ask me to do otherwise that day or perhaps she secretly did want me to be there. The kerosene lamp was placed by the door so that it did not hurt her eyes. The room was darkened and quiet. The only sound was that of her sighs when a spasm occured.

Manorama arrived and stood at the door. The lamp light fell on her face. She could not see anything in the room and stood there wondering what to do next.

My wife was startled enough to clasp my hand and ask, 'Who is that?' Her weakened condition led her to feel alarmed at the sight of a stranger and she repeated, 'Who is that? Do you know who she is?'

For some reason I decided to conceal the truth from her and said immediately, 'I do not know who that is!' But the lie made me feel as if I had been whipped. I corrected myself and said, 'Oh, that is the doctor's daughter!'

She looked at me once, but I could not return the gaze. She then said to the guest, 'Come in,' and to me, she said, 'Hold the light for her.'

Manorama came and sat in the room. The two of them conversed a little. The doctor arrived around this time.

He had brought two bottles of medication with him. He gave the two to my wife and said, 'This blue one is for massaging with and this one is meant for taking internally.

Make sure you do not mix the two, for the blue one is very poisonous if taken internally.'

He also reminded me about the dangers of confusing the two bottles and left them on the bedside table. He called for his daughter when he was about to leave.

She answered her father saying, 'Father, why should I not stay here. There is no other woman here and she is not being looked after properly.'

My wife grew anxious and said, 'No, why should you go out of your way? I have an old maid and she looks after me as her own daughter.'

The doctor smiled and said, 'My sister is like the Lakshmi of our folk lore; she has always looked after others and cannot bear it if others look after her instead.'

When she saw that the doctor was about to leave with his daughter, my wife said, 'Doctor, he has been sitting in this room for a long time, can you take him outside for a walk?'

The doctor said, 'Why not come walking with me to the river bank?'

I protested for a very short while before agreeing to his proposal. Before we left, the doctor cautioned my wife about the two bottles once again.

I dined that night with the doctor. It was late when I returned. I came back to find that my wife was very restless. Stung by repentance, I asked, 'Are you in great pain?'

She could not answer me but looked on in silence, unable to speak.

I immediately sent for the doctor.

The doctor came and looked at her for a long time without being able to detect what was wrong. He then asked, 'Is the pain more? Perhaps she could be massaged with the medicine I gave earlier.'

But when he looked at the bottle where it stood on the table, it was empty.

He asked, 'Did you take this medication by mistake?'

She nodded in silent response, 'Yes.'

The doctor rode home immediately and brought a stomach pump. I sat on her bed like one in a dead faint.

She then drew my head to her breast like a mother comforting a hurt child and attempted to convey her feelings through the touch of her hands. The gentle touch assured me again and again, 'Do not be sad, this is all for your good, you will be happy and I will be able to go happily to my death.'

By the time the doctor returned, my wife had already been released from life as well as all her suffering.

> Dakshinacharan drank some water and said, 'How terribly hot it is!' He then walked out of the room and strode up and down the verandah twice. It was clear that he was not keen to say much but I was extracting what amounted to a confession from his lips. He then came back in and stated, 'I married Manorama and brought her home.'

She did marry me with her father's permission; but when I spoke of my love to her or attempted to gain a place in her heart, she never smiled. How was I to know where her doubts came from?

I began drinking heavily around this time.

One day I was walking in the garden of the Baranagore house with her on an early autumn evening. It was quite dark. The sounds of birds settling down for the night were all silenced. The only sounds were the rustlings in the dark shadowy casuarinas that lined the road.

As soon Manorama grew tired, she lay down upon the white marble seat with her head cushioned on her arms. I came and sat by her.

The place was even darker; what little could be seen of the sky was covered in stars and the insect song rising from the tree's base seemed to be embroidering a fine border to colour in the lowest edges of that vast celestial silence.

I had been drinking that evening as well and was in a rather dream-like state of mind. When my eyes finally grew used to the darkness, the pale shadowy form of the weary woman who lay beneath the tree created an irrepressible emotion within me. I felt that she was merely a shadow and that I would never be able to hold her in my arms.

At that very moment it seemed that the tops of the casuarinas caught fire in the darkness and the wan yellow sliver of a moon rose into the sky above the trees; the light fell upon the white clad woman resting on the white stone. I could not control myself any longer. I drew close enough to clasp her hand in mine and said, 'Manorama, you will not believe me but I do love you. I will never be able to forget you.'

As soon as I said it, I was jolted by the memory that I had said those very words to another not so long ago. A laugh seemed to rise in the night, above the tops of the mimosa and the casuarinas and below the broken yellowed moon in the sky that rang out from the eastern banks of the river to its far banks in the west. I do not know whether it was loud or simply blood curdling. I fainted away immediately and fell to the ground below the marble seat. When I came to my senses, I found I was lying on the bed in my room. My wife asked, 'Why did that suddenly happen to you?'

I trembled violently and said, 'Did you not hear the terrible laughter that shattered the night?'

She smiled and said, 'What laugh? I only heard the flapping wings of a line of birds that flew across the sky. Are you always so easily frightened?'

I now understood that it was the sound of birds in flight as birds arrived to feed on the sand bars of the river from the countries of the north. But I could not remember to be logical when evening fell. When darkness came, I would see the layers of laughter trapped within it that would burst free given the chance. Eventually it came to be that I would not even dare to address Manorama in the evenings.

Then I decided to go on a cruise with Manorama. All my fears evaporated in the river breezes of the winter months. We were so very happy for a few days. Manorama too seemed to open herself to me after days of distance, her guarded heart blossoming under the influence of the beauty that surrounded us.

After the boat had travelled down the Ganga, it entered the Padma river. The great river lay lifeless and tame like a snake in the depths of its winter hibernation. The northern banks were covered in lifeless sands as far as the eyes could see and on the southern banks the mango groves seemed to be waiting in submissive fear at the mercy of the hungry river. The Padma turned every so often as if in sleep and the high banks broke off and collapsed into the currents.

It seemed like a good place to take long walks and the boat was moored.

One day the two of us walked a long way from the boat. As soon as the golden light of the sun faded, the gentle silver glow of the moon rose. When the boundless tide of moonlight had covered the vast white sandy shoal till it stretched to the very horizon, it seemed that we were the sole travellers in that uninhabited, moonlit dreamland. The red shawl that she had wrapped about her slipped off her head and covered her body. When the silence grew dense about us and there was nothing but an endless white void where no compass would have worked, Manorama extended her hand to hold mine and stood close; as if she was submitting herself to me, body and soul in complete trust.

I felt a great joy within me and thought that it was certainly true that love was harder when one was confined indoors. What can hold two humans together if not such a naked unlimited sky? Then I thought that we could be like two travellers with no home to speak of, no doors to walk through and no place to return to, who would hold each other's hands and pass unhindered on unmarked paths with no particular destination in mind.

As we walked we came to a place and saw there was a lake that had formed in the nearby sand—the river had receded and left the water behind.

A long slash of moonlight lay prostrated across the still, unmoving water that was bordered by the desert sand. As we came and stood there, Manorama looked at me. Her face was illuminated by moonlight as I lifted it to mine and kissed her.

Somewhere in the emptiness of that sandy stretch someone spoke sombrely three times, 'Who is that? Who is that? Who is that?'

I started at the sound and my wife trembled, but we both realised our folly immediately as the sounds were neither human nor supernatural but the cries of waterfowl from the sandbars. They had woken up at the appearance of people in their safe secluded haven.

The two of us returned to the boat quickly, having experienced fear. We went to bed at night and Manorama fell asleep immediately as she was exhausted. And I lay by her watching as an apparition appeared by the bed and stood pointing at Manorama with a long skeletal finger. It whispered to me again and again, 'Who is she? Who is that?'

I quickly woke and lit a match. The apparition disappeared instantly, but as it went, it shook my bed and the boat and froze the very blood in my overheated body with the sounds of loud laughter. The terrible sound seemed to leave the river behind, cross the sand islands across its broad breast, across the sleeping villages and towns on the far side of the river till it rose and mingled into the infinite space around us, fading gradually, till it transcended mortal life and then grew softer and softer till a sound as fine as a needle remained. I had neither heard nor imagined that such a sound could exist; it seemed that the sky was trapped within my brain and that the sound trapped within could not escape those confines despite all the distance it had travelled. Eventually when it became unbearable, I thought I would sleep if the lights were doused but as soon as I did that and came back to bed, I heard the disembodied voice speak out of the darkness, 'Who is that? Who is she? Do you know who she is?' My heart beat to the question, 'Who is she? Who is she?' Even the clock face in the silent boat on that night seemed to come alive and point its hands at Manorama and ask, 'Who is that? Who is she? Do you know who she is?'

> As he spoke his face grew pale and his voice seemed to choke. I touched his arm and said, 'Have a sip of water.' The kerosene lamp began to flicker and went out. I now saw that it was getting lighter outside. A crow cawed and another bird whistled its call. The squeaking of a buffalo-drawn cart rose from the street that passed by the house. The expression on his face changed completely and there was no sign of fear any more.
>
> He seemed very ashamed and a little angry with me because he had told me a great deal about himself under the effects of the imagined fears that overcame him at night.
>
> At midnight again came the knock at my door; 'Doctor, doctor!'

(Nishithe – Golpo Guchcho)

Some Time Away

Why not while some time away?

How do I convey
Where I wish I could be.
Where the Shirish trees grow in dense perfumed closeness
And bee wings shimmer all day.

Where clouds float in a distance all of their own,
Where the rush of water speaks to a distracted mind
Where all questions come to cease,
As the evening star rises.

Memories do not hum in empty rooms
Nor keep sleep away on rainy nights.

Where the mind becomes
A great tree in silent watch, over cattle grazed fields
By little used village paths.

Where one may pause to sit a while
Or play a flute full of yearning,
As a retinue escorting a new bride,
Waits in the heat of mid-day.

On dark moonless nights
Listless lunar light clings to the embrace
Of shadows serenaded by insect song.

Comings and goings night and day
No eager hold on anything
Nor bruised pride over leaving.

There the stars of the night illumine dreams
Then give way to pearly dawn light
As they leave for places unknown.

Chuti, Punascha – 15th September 1932

In Sickness

I do not believe in my exploits
Knowing that the waves of Time
Daily break them
Into nothingness little by little.
I believe in myself.

Each day filling my vessel
With all the beauty of this everyday world
I have drunk my fill.
The love of every moment
Has collected in it.

It has not crushed with grief,
Nor darkened with dust
The artistry of that vessel.

This I know, when I leave
The stage of daily life,
The flowers will give witness in seasons to come
I have loved this world.

This love is the truth, the gift of this life.
When I say farewell
This truth will burn bright and deny death.

(The 26th verse of Rogshojya – Udayan, 28th November 1940)

The Offering

The last shadows of my day
Blend into the strains of Multan—
Its whisper will remain forever,
Its meaning though forgotten.

When the tired traveller sits
To rest by the roadside
The sad strains of that tune
Will touch him,
As he listens with bowed head,
In silence he will know this,
Even if he knows nothing else—
'In a forgotten age, for a precious moment
Someone had lived once,
We have not found him
But he has found us.'

(10th verse of Rogshojya – Jorasanko, 13th November 1940)

The Handmaiden's Prayer

Emperor Bimbisara
Revered the Buddha and was given
A relic by the Enlightened One.
In the palace garden serene,
He built a reliquary to complete the scene.
A wondrous *stupa* from stone was carved
A glorious ode to the treasure within.

In the evening each queen and princess,
Came purified in mind and dress
Flowers heaped in pleasing array,
Upon plates of shining gold.
Around the great dome,
They lit with their own hands,
Shimmering lamps in numbers untold.

When Ajaatshatru became ruler
Following his father to his seat,
He washed away the old beliefs
With the blood of layman and priest—
He cast into the fires dread,
All telling of the Buddha's creed.
Summoning the royal women, he said
You must understand this new rule,
The Vedas, the Brahmins and the King are supreme!
Worship no one else under my regime
Forgetting this will earn my displeasure
And a most severe censure.

That day as the sun set over the city
A gentle young girl, her name Sreemati
Having washed in the pure and cool waters
Adorned a plate with votive flowers.
Came and stood meekly before the queen
Her eyes downcast, demure her mien.

Trembling in fear, the queen exclaimed,
'Do you not recall what was proclaimed?
Ajaatsatru has sent the word
Anyone that prays to the Buddha our Lord,
Will die most painfully upon the stake,
Or be banished forever in shame.'

From there she went with measured steps
To the princess Amita's rooms.

Where she.was seated before a mirror golden,
As she sat plaiting her tresses long and silken.
She was painting her parting with care
So that the vermilion red would glow in her hair.

Sreemati's coming made her hand shake,
And the line of red uncertain make.
She said, 'Fool, what kind of courage is this?
You come with these offerings remiss,
If someone sees you, or the king finds out,
You risk gravest harm without a doubt!'

By the glow of the setting sun,
Sitting by a window left open
Princess Shukla was all alone.
Reading poetry on her own,
She started as she heard anklets sing
And looked at the door, eyes questioning.

Seeing Sreemati, she put her book down
And hurried to her side in fear,
She whispered carefully in her ear,
'Who knows not of the king's decree?
And I know what I today see.
Why must you still want to rush head long
Towards death inevitable and prolonged!'

Sreemati went from door to door
Carrying her offerings upon a plate.

'Women of this city' she implored
'The hour draws nigh for the Lord to be adored'—
Some were afraid upon hearing her call
Others cursed her for her folly.

The last light of day fades
From the great city walls.
The roads grow empty and darkness shrouded
The sounds of the day are slowly silenced—
A bell peals out ushering the faithful
To the ancient palace temple.

In the clear darkness of that autumn night
A million stars burn steady and bright.
The horns are sounded at the gates in warning,
As prisoners start a prayer for the evening,
'The king and his council have met'
The guard calls, voice gruff in threat.

Suddenly a murmur rose
Amongst the sentries that night—
As they looked at the darkened garden.
Around the base of the neglected shrine,
What are those burning in flickering rows?
A chain of votive lamps all alight.

Sword at the ready, a town guard
Rushed immediately at her
Asking, 'Who are you, wretch,

Praying for death to deliver you quick!'
Sweet came the reply, 'Sreemati,
Buddha's handmaiden am I.'

That day upon the cold white stone
Dripped red blood from a blameless one
On that calm and clear autumn night
In the silence of the palace garden
A single votive glowing bright
Was put out in abrupt anger.

(Pujarini – 3rd October 1899)

Your Conch Shell

There lies your conch shell in the dust,
How am I supposed to bear it?
The light and air have grown stale
What kind of destiny is this?
Come who will, carrying the flag,
Come, lend your voice to this song,
Come who will, on winged feet,
Come along, those of you without fear.
Look there lies forsaken
Upon the dust, the conch shell of peace.

I was going to offer my prayers
With flowers arranged as my gift
I wish to find at the end of the day

Somewhere a haven of peace.
This time the wounds that bleed within
I had hoped to heal,
And wash away all signs of wear
I would become renewed and clean.
But what should I see cast upon the dust
But your great conch shell of peace.

Is this how one lights the flame of sacrifice?
Is this how the day must end for me?
Will all the flowers be turned blood red?
Alas the flowers of purity and youth.
I had thought that all the wars
Were finally over for me,
And all my debts paid to this life,
Now I would finally be with you.
And yet I find I am called to war
By the silence of your conch.

With the touch of youth
Then bring me to life.
Set aflame my spirits
In joyous response to your call.
Drive away the darkness
Awaken the skies
In every unseeing direction
With a hint of the horrors to come.
I will lift with my hands
Your conch shell of victory.

I know I have been asleep
But that will be no more.
I know that like the blinding rain
The weapons will ring within
Some come racing, eager to join
Some beat their breasts with sighs,
Nightmares will shake
Those asleep in bed.
For today once again we sound
Your great conch shell in battle.

You looked upon me in pity
When I begged for respite
Now I will have nothing less
Than you dressing me in your armour bright.
Let there come whatever may,
I will not budge from my stand,
For your pain will strike in me
The victory drums in delight
I will give all that I can
In return I claim for my own
Your conch shell of peace that lay upon the dust.

(Bolaka 4 – Ramgarh, 26th May 1914)

Unfortunate Land

My unfortunate land, those that you have daily disdained,
One day you must find yourself equal to them.
And those from whom you have withheld
The very right to a human existence,
Making them stand by and watch your uncaring gaze
You will be pulled down till you are on their plane.

Denying yourself the kindness of human touch
Daily you have defiled the spirit within the human soul.
One day the terrible anger of fate
Will make certain that famine
Will force you to fight for your share of what others throw
to you.
You will be their equal in every way.

Where you banished them, far from your throne
There sits your strength, forever gone.
Crushed underfoot
It languishes in cruel dust—
You must descend to that depth, if you wish to save yourself.
That day you must become equal to them all.

The ones that you have cast down, they will pull you into the abyss
The ones you left behind hold you back with all their might.
In the darkness of ignorance
Remain those that you discarded.
But that blight grows covering the way to redemption,
You will be their equal in shamed existence.

Centuries of shame have forced your head down
But still you will not honour the living gods
Still you do not lower your eyes
Do you never see?
There on the dust sits the god of the meek.
There, where you must become their equal in every way.

Do you not see that messenger of death
That stands at your door marking it with a curse?
If you do not call them all,
But keep them removed and apart,
Harshly distancing them with pride.
In death your ashes shall equally mingle with theirs.

(Gitanjali, 108th verse – 4th July 1910)

Africa

In the restless tides of that primordial dawn
When the creator himself despaired of crafting you
And struck angrily at the fresh clay again and again,
In that hour of impatience and rage
The arms of the brave seas
Plucked you from the clasp of the lands of the East
Removing you far from them all, Africa
To bind you within cages of great trees standing guard
Where miserly light illumined your fate
There in silent wait you bided your time,
Reading the mysteries of the unreachable,
And learning the incomprehensible signs hidden in land, sea
and sky
That magic that is beyond any seen in nature

Wove spells through your unconscious mind.
You mocked the terrible
Dressed as a grotesque lampooning of the fierce,
You wished to defeat fear itself by donning it as disguise
Alas, shadowed beauty,
How well you hid yourself under veil of night
Your human form secreted away
From those whose eyes shower contempt,
They came with shackles forged from cruel iron
Those who bear claws sharper than the wolves that roam the land,
Then came the ones who make trade with human coin
Those whose pride blinds them, their hearts darker than your sunless forests.
The naked hunger of the civilized
Stripping them down to their inner shameless brutality.
In the forests drenched by your wordless cries
The very soil sullied by your blood and sweat;
Under the feet of their hob-nailed boots,
Mutilated your flesh
Marks forever your maligned history.

At that very moment in their own lands
Church bells rang out in glorious worship
At morning and evensong, in the name of an all merciful God;
While their children played in each mother's lap;
And poets raised their wondrous tunes
In praise of all things bright and beautiful.

When today on the western horizon
Sunset holds it breath in fear of a new storm,
When the beasts ride out of secret caves
And sounds of ill omen declare the beginning of day's end,
Come forth, Oh poet of change
Stand by the last ray of this evening's sun
Where this unfortunate woman waits,
And say, 'Forgive me!'
In the midst of fierce delirium,
Let that be the final reparation made by your civilization.

(Africa – Santiniketan, 10th February 1937)

Why, I ask

Lord, you have sent your messengers through the ages
To this pitiless world
They have said 'Forgive thy enemies,' they have said 'Love them—
Defeat this bitter hatred that lurks within you'.

They are to be revered, they are to be remembered,
and yet today, in this terrible hour
I have turned them away from my door with polite rejection
For I have seen the horror of insidious malice wreak vengeance
On the meek, under cover of this delusive night
And witnessed the voice of justice silenced, doomed to weep
In the face of tyranny

For I have also seen the senseless death of innocent youth
maddened by turmoil
As they beat their heads in impotent rage against the stony
walls of Fate.

My voice is stilled today, muted lies my flute,
This darkness confines
My world under a weight of nightmarish proportions
That is why I need to ask of you today,
Have you forgiven them, Oh Lord, those that
make rank the air?

Do you love them too, those that have darkened the world?

(Proshno – January 1932)

Gandhari's Supplication

Dhritarashtra: *The blind king of the Kurus*

Duryodhana: *His eldest son, the Kaurava prince*

Gandhari: *Dhritarashtra's queen and mother to a hundred Kauravas.*

Duryodhana: I pay you my respects, Oh Father!
Dhritarashtra: Oh Wicked One,
Have you achieved your aim?
Duryodhana: I have achieved supremacy.
Dhritarashtra: Are you now happy?
Duryodhana: I am victorious.
Dhritarashtra: Where is the happiness in winning this undivided kingdom?
Duryodhana: I did not ask for happiness!
Victory, victory was my objective and I have achieved that!

Inconsequential moments of happiness do not satisfy the warrior's hunger,
Oh Leader of the Kurus—the fierce taste of victory
Churned from the oceans of my jealous mind!
This I have drunk!
Am I happy? No Father, today I have gained ascendancy.
Father, I *was* happy, when we remained confined with the Pandavas,
As though a blemish upon the fair face of the moon
In idle, impotent placidity.
I *was* happy, when the thunder of the Pandava bows
Kept anxious enemies from my door.
I *was* happy, when the Pandavas brought the wealth of their conquered domains to us
Sharing them in brotherly affection,
The days passed in entertainment and humor.
I *was* happy, the praise of the Pandavas daily echoing in my ears,
The reflected brilliance of the Pandava exploits making more apparent
What we Kauravas lacked.
I *was* happy, all pride extinguished, to live in the shadow of Pandava glory
As a toad lying undisturbed in the gloom of a well.
Today, when the vanquished Pandavas leave for their forest exile,
I am not happy, today I am SUPREME.
Dhritarashtra: Shame on your hatred for your brothers!
Have you forgotten that the Pandavas and the Kauravas had the same grandfather?

Duryodhana: That is what I cannot forget—
One grandfather yet unequal in every aspect
In wealth, in fame and in prowess!
If they were but distant, there would have been no anger.
The pale moon does not envy the brilliance of the sun in
The mid day sky;
But two suns will never share the honor of crowning the
Eastern horizon at dawn!
Today there is no more conflict, today I am victorious,
Today I stand alone.
Dhritarashtra: Petty Jealousy!
She is poisonous indeed!
Duryodhana: Jealousy is not petty! She is magnificent!
The religion of the great! Two forest giants do not
Grow within the same space, yet millions of blades
Of grass grow jostled side by side;
Numerous stars form a celestial brotherhood—
Yet there is but one sun and one moon
Today when the pale Pandava moon sets
Behind the distant forest,
Today the Kuru sun shines in glory—
Today I am victorious!
Dhritarashtra: Truth lies vanquished today!
Duryodhana: The idea of Truth differs between the rulers
And the ruled; they live at peace with equals
In the bonds of friendship and mutual interest.
But the King stands alone, a God unto himself,
Thus his only equals are his greatest enemies, insurmountable
odds,

The unknown future, unseen danger
The fear of losing power, fame and fortune that
Clouds each waking hour and drives away sleep,
The loss of wealth.
Ordinary men share all they have happily to peacefully coexist.
That is not the way of the King; he grows weak if he shares his sceptre
If a King is not seen from afar, his proud head raised above all others,
in the view of many, how will his subjects obey him?
How will his rule be established?
The King's code does not allow for brotherly love, nor excuses friendship,
It only worships victory.
Oh King! That is why today, I am fulfilled
Today I am victorious.
Today the five peaks of Pandava prowess lie prostrated at my feet.
Dhritarashtra: You won in a false game of cards, you call that victory!
Shameless pride!
Duryodhana: Father, we play with the weapons we have been given!
Unequal though we may be to a tiger in claw and fang, what man hesitates
To kill the beast with an arrow? To surrender to death without prior thought in battle
These are but the actions of a fool! In war to win is the only aim,
That I have achieved today, I am victorious Father!

Yes, today I am proud!
Dhritarashtra: Today you are the victor which is why
Shameful cries rend both earth and sky.
Duryodhana: Condemnation! No longer do I fear it,
I will suffocate all condemnation.
I will silence this clamorous city
Crush its tongue and its audacity
Underfoot; 'Duryodhana the sinner!'
'Duryodhana connives!', 'Duryodhana the low!'
Long have I heard this without uttering a word.
Today I pledge by this sceptre of mine, Oh King,
I will make them say this instead—
'Duryodhana is King'. Duryodhana does not suffer
Criticism, discussion; Duryodhana forges
His fate with his own hands!
Dhritarashtra: Son, hear me,
To banish criticism from the tongues of people,
Is to ensure that it spreads
Its roots, in the darkness of people's minds.
It poisons them daily.
Allowing it to spend itself in effusive speech
Exhausts criticism; do not allow it
To build its strength in silence enforced
In the secret fortresses of the soul.
With the promise of love, calm it
Imprison it, charm the snake of protest
With the flute song of smiling deceit.
Duryodhana: Unexpressed condemnation,
Does nothing to the honour of a King;

I do not fear that; I do not care
That I am not loved, but audacity is unwelcome
Oh King! Love is voluntary,
Even the poorest can gift love—
Let them give that love freely to tame cats,
To stray dogs at their door, and to the Pandavas—
I do not need that love. I shall be feared;
That is my right as ruler, as King.
I demand victory, by destroying any pride
Felt by those who deserve it.
Listen to my plea
Father—for long has your throne
Been surrounded by my critics daily,
Like a wall of thorns creating
A barrier most cruel between you and me,
They have daily sung the praises of my enemy,
And our calumny—this is how
Father, we have been banished from your love forever.
This is how, Father, from childhood
We have been rendered weak—the source
Of fatherly affection dammed, we became
The weaker tributary, lifeless, immobile
Prevented from achieving glory; the Pandavas growing,
Untrammeled, unrestrained. If hereafter,
Father, you do not banish the band of critics
That surrounds your throne, Sanjoy, Vidura
Grandfatherly Bhishma, if you allow
Them to continue, in the guise of wise, right advice
To daily condemn, correct and undermine

At every step the carriage of kingly duties,
And stay my sceptre,
Interrupting at every chance kingly concourse,
And shame the crown,
Then forgive me father—I have no use for
This throne of thorns—Oh King,
Let me exchange my fate with the Pandavas
Give up my kingdom and go on exile instead.
Dhritarashtra: Alas, conceited son! Were it that
My love for you had been less
As was advised most strongly by able friends
It would have been right.
I have joined the forces of evil, lost all sense
So much love! I am your ruination,
So much love! I have lit a deadly fire
That eats away at the ancient Kuru family tree
Still, son you rebuke me for not loving you enough?
You desired a deadly snake for the gem on its brow,
I caught that for you with these hands of mine
I am blind! I have been thus within and without
Forever—as we walk together into this deadly storm
Friends entreat me to stop, the unholy animals of the night
Screech their calls, at each step
The path grows ever constricted, approaching evil
Makes my skin crawl, yet still with unshaken hand
I gather you to my breast with terrible love,
And speed blindly into the gaping maw of disaster,
Maddened by foolishness, laughing,
Our path lit by the ill-fated glow of comets.

Our only companion, our Fate
Thunderbolt in hand—
No foresight, no restraint behind
We are bound in a downward spin
To certain downfall. Suddenly will you
Realise, as the mighty hand of God falls
Do not doubt in your father's love till then
Do not release this embrace chilling, till then
Steal everything you desire
Be victorious, be at peace, be a King,
Alone, exalted. Hark, you all
Play the songs of Kuru victory, fly our pennants high
Today in this celebration of victory, we do not invite
Right, truth, brother, or friend, nay—
Not Vidura, not Bhishma, nor Sanjoy,
We will not hear condemnation or cries of shame from subjects
The guardian spirit of our dynasty neither—
The only two invited will be you and me,
A blind father and his son unseeing,
And Death—a father's love
And the curse of God, no one else.
The spy: King, the Brahmins have forsaken
The worship of fire and the other gods
Evening prayers forgotten, they wait
For the Pandavas, by the side of the road.
Not one person remains at home, all the
Pleasure houses are closed; even as evening
Draws close, no bells ring, nor conch shells sound
No lamps are lit in the temple of Shiva.

The populace mourns as they move as one,
All walking towards the main gates of the city.
Duryodhana: They do not know
Duryodhana has awakened. Ignorant and unfortunate!
You do not know, yet your doom approaches fast and furious,
Today ruler will meet subject in a union, at once
Intimate and cruel! Let me see how long
This is sustained. The ultimate insolence of the ruled,
The futile brandishing of a fangless snake's hood.
A call to arms from disarmed pride.

The gatekeeper approaches
Gatekeeper: Great King, Queen Gandhari
Wishes to pay her respects to you
Dhritarashtra: I have been awaiting her presence.
Duryodhana: Father, I must leave then.
Dhritarashtra: Yes, run, escape. Alas! How will you
Bear the eyes of your chaste mother upon your face
Her glances as ferocious as lightening
You who are afraid of virtue! You have nothing
To be ashamed of in my presence!
Gandhari: I have a request that I must place before you,
I beseech you, Oh husband!
Save us.
Dhritarashtra: Have your pleas ever gone unfulfilled, dearest?
Gandhari: Cast him aside now.
Dhritarashtra: Who should I cast aside, Oh Queen?
Gandhari: That ignorant, whose misdeeds abrade and
Sharpen the keen edge of the sword of Justice

He must be cast aside.
Dhritarashtra: Who is this person? Where does he live?
Just once utter his name.
Gandhari: Duryodhana, our son.
Dhritarashtra: I must cast him aside?
Gandhari: This I submit
At your feet.
Dhritarashtra: A terrible supplication, Gandhari!
Queen Mother!
Gandhari: Is this then my wish alone
Oh Kaurava? The great Kuru Kings of the past
Are praying for the same from the highest heaven
Oh King of men! Cast aside, cast aside now the one
Whose misdeeds have seen the Goddess of Prosperity and well-being
Weep as she awaits her moment of departure,
Day and night.
Dhritarashtra: Justice will see him punished
For he has sinned against that alone,
I am his father.
Gandhari: Am I not his mother? Burdened with his weight within my womb
Did I not bear him close to my watchful heart?
Did not the tender love of my soul gush forth
As the milk of maternal kindness from these breasts of mine
As I gazed in wonder upon his innocent newly formed face?
Just as fruit clings to a branch, did he not
For many years hold me close,
With his tiny arms drawing

His smiles from my smiles, his words from my speech,
His very life from my life force? And yet I say to you, Oh King!
Cast aside that son of mine, cast aside Duryodhana today.

Dhritarashtra: What shall I have after that is done?
Gandhari: Your sense of justice.
Dhritarashtra: What will justice give you?
Gandhari: Sorrow and more sorrow
How will I exist for the rest of my days?
My son's happiness and a kingdom won at the cost of my conscience;
Twin thorns impaled within my heart's embrace?
Dhritarashtra: Alas, my beloved
Once, overcome by conscience, I had returned the pawned Kingdoms of
The Pandavas who had been vanquished at a game of dice
The very next moment fatherly love spoke against it
A hundred times in my ear, 'What have you done?'
No one survives riding the twin prows of good and evil. When the
Sons of Kuru have descended into the currents of evil,
It is futile to seek truce with Justice,
Evil comes asking Evil for help.
What have you done, you wretch, you old imbecile,
Influenced by weak hesitation? The scars of denigration
Do not fade even if their kingdom you return
From the minds of the Pandavas, just new fuel
Added to old conflagration. To arm the dishonored
With the weapons of power is to welcome death.

Do not release the able after striking gentle blows;
Crush them! Do not play games
With sin; once you have greeted it,
Welcome it and accept it completely.
Thus did evil thought in the guise of filial love
Prick my ears with words whispered
Piercing and provoking. Again
Returned the Pandavas; this time the dice rolled
Banishing them to the forests for longer. Alas Justice,
Alas my instincts! Who will understand
The ways of the world?

Gandhari: Righteousness is not something we can own
Oh King, nor a little bridge that leads somehow to happiness.
Righteousness leads back to itself. I am but an ignorant woman,
How do I explain the tenets of faith to you?
You know it all. The Pandavas will go to the forest,
They will not return even if entreated, as they are bound by their own vows.
Now this vast Kingdom is yours alone
King of the world, denounce your son now.
Through the infliction of pain upon the blameless
Do not satisfy your need for happiness; do not turn the creed of truth
Away from Puru's palace. Unbearable sorrow
From today, Righteous king, you must accept
And share with me.
Dhritarashtra: Alas Queen!
Your advice is just and your words severe.

Gandhari: Having chosen the honeyed fruit of death
Our son dances in celebration; Beguiled by your false affection
Do not allow him to enjoy that;
Wrest it from him, throw it far; make him weep if he chooses.
This Kingdom gained by deceit, these coffers swollen by sin
Leaving these let him too be exiled,
And bear the same burden of grief
As the deprived Pandavas.
Dhritarashtra: The rules belong to Providence
He is watchful; his sceptre of truth
Raised at all times; Oh Calm one,
In his Kingdom he will do what is right,
I am but a father.
Gandhari: You are King, a King of kings
The left hand of God; the preservation of right
Is yours to execute. I ask of you,
If any subject of yours dragged
A chaste helpless woman from her home
And defamed her for no reason
What would you do with him?
Dhritarashtra: Exile!
Gandhari: Then today at your feet, on behalf of all women,
In tearful supplication, I ask for justice.
Our son Duryodhana is guilty, Lord!
You, King, are witness to this. Men fight men,
Self interest colours their disputes, the meaning of
Which I do not comprehend; Divisiveness,
Politics and many others are the reason. Only men know
The policies in the minds of other men. Force pitted against force,

Many are the intrigues that arise in this combat.
Tact against artifice; we stay afar,
With our own duties in the peace of our quarters.
The one who brought the flames of rivalry inside,
The one who poured the poison of jealousy
From the disputes without leaving behind
His quarrels with men,
Entering the chamber of helpless women,
Defiled with his sinful rough hands
The virtuous body of a woman.
War with the husband not enough;
He attacks the wife to extract unjust revenge,
He is not just a brute, he is a coward.
King, what would you do with him? If sin had
Taken root in the pure lineage of Puru
I would bear it; but Lord, with a mother's pride
I have hoped that I had given birth
To brave sons. Alas
That day when helpless Panchali's screams of terror
Shook the very foundations of this palace of stone
Ashamed, aghast, agonized, I hastened to see
From the window, cackling evilly in their own great court
Gandhari's sons, disrobing her, my conscience knows
That day was shattered for life
Any shreds of maternal pride. Kuru Kings,
Where has chivalry gone leaving this land!
You all, great leaders, as immobile as statues
Sat there, looking at each other
Some smiled, some jested in glee

Whispering, while you, a stilled sword,
A thunderbolt spent of all its lightning
A sleeping king, listen Oh King
To this appeal. Banish a mother's shame,
Return to the path of the brave, restore her humbled chastity;
Pay your respects
To denigrated truth,
And cast aside Duryodhana.

Dhritarashtra: You strike futile blows upon
My unrepentant weary heart
Oh Queen!
Gandhari: Is my pain not a hundred-fold more? Lord, when the oppressed
And the oppressor suffer a punishment equally
That is the fairest judgment of all. When the heart feels naught
For the punishment it metes out, it becomes merely an exertion of
Strength against the meek. The punishment
You cannot give your son, do not, I pray, enforce it upon others
The one that you punish may not be yours but is son to another surely.
You will sin against them both.
Judge, I have heard that the Creator
Is a father to us all and daily he does his duty, meting out justice
With his own hands; he gives us pain and feels it in equal measure.
That entitles him to play judge.
Ignorant woman though I am, this is my own
Realisation. If you forgive your son's sins

Today without hesitation and thought, then eternally
All your judgment, your punishments
As an upholder of justice, in the failed exercise of duty;
They will return as admonishment, retribution for the sins
Of our son. Abandon still the
Sinful Duryodhan!
Dhritarashtra: Dearest, retract your words! Withdraw them!
I cannot tear these bonds of love. Your
Righteous words rain dully upon my steely resolve. God has abandoned my sinful son
That is why I cannot cast him aside.
I alone remain, in his camp. How do I forsake a son
Who has plunged without thought into furious turmoil?
Without hope of succour,
I still must clasp him to my breast and plunge into the same maelstrom,
I submit to the same destruction and share in his misfortune,
I take on half of what retribution is due to him.
That is my consolation in this hour, now that there remains
No more time to judge right from wrong, or time to repent,
No way out, whatever was bound to, has happened,
The results will be whatever they are ordained to be.

Dhritarashtra departs
Gandhari: My unsettled heart
Calm down. With bowed head
Wait for the final judgement of the day
Patiently. That day when time awakens at the
End of that terrible night and

Redeems itself; that is a terrible day indeed.
Just as heat scorches the calm restful air
Into waking up, transforming itself into sudden storm,
Attacking its own immobility
Like a blinded scorpion, stinging itself with terrible vengeance,
A burning lightning strike; when truth seeks redemption
We fear it as our nemesis.
Bow your head, incline it, and prostrate yourself
Before that terrible anger; the sounds of the passage of its wheels
Resonate as thunder peals from the distance. Place your
Weary tormented soul in its path. Let the torn bloodied petals
Of your heart be as an offering of silenced, astounded prayer.
Then, when the sky swirls with dust and the earth trembles,
Wails arise suddenly, carried upwards on the grim winds.
Alas woman, unprotected and friendless
Consort of the brave warrior, mother to the unvanquished
Alas! The desolation, the remorse! When gently
You fall upon the dust with bowed head,
Eyes, unseeing against impending doom and then, Hail!
The inevitable ending, unspeaking and merciless
Terrible yet compassionate that peace! Hail
Stern faced and most compassionate pity!
Hail the tremendous deliverance from all dispute!
The ashen pallor of ultimate release upon the funeral pyre!

Bhanumati enters

Bhanumati: Indumati, Porobhritey, lift up these
Jewels and treasure beyond compare.

Gandhari: Child, gently,

What great celebration is this in the palaces of Kuru?
Where do you hasten in this new finery,
Daughter-in-law of mine?
Bhanumati: The auspicious moment of welcome defeat approaches
For our enemies.
Gandhari: When you make enemies out of your own blood,
Your very soul is your foe, Truth opposes you too,
Unstoppable its onslaught. Where did you gather these
New ornaments, Kind One?
Bhanumati: The five brave husbands of Panchali by the virtue of their strength,
brought for her the treasures of every conquered land, covering her in the gold
And silver of the defeated. Long did she wear them with pride, the jewels
Glittering like a million shards that pierced our hearts, we wives of Kuru.
Today she had to hand them over, dressing me with her own hands,
She now is bound for her forest exile.
Gandhari: Alas! Ignorant child, you have not learned?
Still such pride over that wrongly won treasure?
How terrible you look as you prepare for ultimate ruin?
Do you not feel these jewels sear your skin with an unholy heat
Like a comet heralding the end of days?
The jeweled head piece like a lightning strike that cleaves your head asunder!
As I look upon you I tremble with

Fear, my soul fills with sorrow, my ears ring with
The tinkling of your ornaments like
The maddened cymbals of an enraged Shiva.
Bhanumati: Mother, but we are warrior women, misfortune
Is not for us to fear. Sometimes victory, sometimes defeat,
Sometime high in the midday sky, sometimes setting,
The sun of a warrior's glory waxes and wanes.
As wives of warriors, Mother, that I know to be truth
Living as I do in the embrace of fear without a care,
Oblivious to impending doom. If adversity should come,
Let it, I laugh in the face of my contrary fate.
Mother, I assure you I do know how to die,
Just as I have learned how to live from you.
Gandhari: Daughter! This ill fate is not yours alone to bear,
When misfortune arrives in fearful array, it will take all.
It will satisfy its hunger, and the world will mourn.
The tears of many a widow will mingle with the lost blood of many a warrior;
Ornaments tumble from bereft limbs like a multitude of fallen blooms,
After an ill wind has swept through a beautiful grove.
Child, do not break these bridges.
Do not raise the flags of revolt under the guise of play.
Today is not a day of celebration in this house.
Do not deck yourself with the misfortunes of your own flesh and blood.
Curb your pride! Control yourself,
From this day forth, purify yourself with fasting,
Undress your hair and pray to the gods.

Do not shame your Fate with such proud display on a day of unfortunate gain.
Cast aside these jewels, this blood red robe;
Call for the trumpets to stop sounding notes of victory and royal pomp;
Go to the chamber of sacrificial fire and with the priests;
Let us await the coming of Retribution with unwavering faith.

Bhanumati exits and the Pandavas enter with Draupadi
Yudhishtira: Mother, we come to ask for your blessings
As we leave this palace.
Gandhari: The sun of good fortune
Will rise with twice the brilliance at the end of this night of sorrow
Sons of mine! May the wind grant you strength,
The sun his fierce spirit, the earth her forbearance,
I wish all of these for you, avowed to pain as you are!
Prosperity will remain in the midst of want disguised,
And will accompany you in all that you do, without fanfare
Gleaning from pain, a treasure without end. May you live
Your exile free from fear. May this needless punishment
Add fire to the spirit that burns within
As a flame burnishes shining gold.
That grave sorrow will be your great support,
Truth will remain in your thrall, when your time comes
Your debts to discharge, who will stand before you?
Neither celestial beings nor men!
All the wrongs wrought by my sons,
May my blessings negate them all

For you are greater to me than them! Your wrongful treatment
Will surely evoke compassion from the greatest of depths.

Embracing Draupadi, the Pandava Queen:
My child, you seem as an uprooted golden vine
My eclipsed moon, just once
Raise your head, heed what I say:
The one that has vilified you will forever
Remain ill famed in this world; despised eternally.
Your shame is shared by women worldwide,
The torment of a good woman at the hands of a coward
Go child, accompanying your husband, with unclouded face
Transform the forest into heaven; be happy in the midst of sorrow.
Daughter of mine, sharing your husband's unbearable pain
Transform it into the glory of faith in fidelity.
Here in the palace, day and night, abound a thousand pleasures;
There in the forest, you will be alone, the sole source of
Every pleasure, all companionship, all the wealth,
All consolation, every shelter,
Respite from exhaustion, provider of peace and healing.
The blessing of plenty in their days of hardship,
The promise of a better dawn, shining beacon in the dark times.
You will be alone; receiving and giving all love and care,
Mother, wife and queen!
The sanctity of your pure spirit will prevail, proud and inviolate.

(Gandharir Abedon – February, 1898)